HIDDEN DYNAMICS

HIDDEN DYNAMICS

How Emotions Affect Business Performance
& How You Can Harness Their Power
for Positive Results

Faith Ralston, Ph.D.

amacom
American Management Association
New York • Atlanta • Boston • Chicago • Kansas City • San Francisco • Washington, D. C.
Brussels • Mexico City • Tokyo • Toronto

This publication is designed to provide accurate and authoritative information in regard to the subject matter covered. It is sold with the understanding that the publisher is not engaged in rendering legal, accounting, or other professional service. If legal advice or other expert assistance is required, the services of a competent professional person should be sought.

Library of Congress Cataloging-in-Publication Data

Ralston, Faith.
    Hidden dynamics : how emotions affect business performance & how
you can harness their power for positive results / Faith Ralston.
        p.   cm.
    Includes bibliographical references and index.
    ISBN 0-8144-0272-0
    1. Management—Psychological aspects—Problems, exercises, etc.
2. Personnel management—Psychological aspects—Problems, exercises,
etc.   I. Title.
HD30.413.R35   1995
658.3'001'9—dc20   95-3940
                                                                   CIP

Printing number

10   9   8   7   6   5   4   3   2

To my
father,
who was a minister,
and my dad,
who was a man

Contents

List of Action Exercises

Chapter 1

Exercise 1: Clarifying Beliefs About Feelings
Exercise 2: Recognizing Changes in Business Behaviors and Attitudes
Exercise 3: Taking Action to Build Community

Chapter 2

Exercise 1: Clarifying Your Real Feelings
Exercise 2: Discovering What Others See When You're Upset
Exercise 3: Becoming Aware of Your Beliefs About Anger
Exercise 4: Learning to Listen

Chapter 3

Exercise 1: Learning From Mistakes—Level One
Exercise 2: Learning From Mistakes—Level Two
Exercise 3: Unearthing Solutions to Workplace Problems

Chapter 4

Exercise 1: Addressing Hidden Agendas
Exercise 2: Unraveling Entangled Decision Making

Chapter 5
    Exercise 1:   Identifying Hot Buttons
    Exercise 2:   Defusing Hot Buttons
    Exercise 3:   Accepting Responsibility for Your Own Life

Chapter 6
    Exercise 1:   Identifying Symptoms of Corporate Craziness
    Exercise 2:   Defining Workplace Values
    Exercise 3:   Improving Work Relationships

Chapter 7
    Exercise 1:   Identifying Changes in Roles and Expectations
    Exercise 2:   Understanding the Dynamics of Manager/
                  Employee Relationships

Chapter 8
    Exercise 1:   Making Career Changes
    Exercise 2:   Finding Your Joy
    Exercise 3:   Supporting Career Development

Chapter 9
    Exercise 1:   Troubleshooting When Change Is Failing
    Exercise 2:   Dealing With Change

Chapter 10
    Exercise 1:   Clarifying the Manager's Role
    Exercise 2:   Receiving Feedback on Management Style
    Exercise 3:   Practicing Facilitation Skills
    Exercise 4:   Applying Facilitation Skills

Acknowledgments

I am grateful to the following individuals for their trust, encouragement, and enthusiasm as I wrote this book:

Janice Siedsma Kennedy, for being my highest jumping cheerleader

Elleva Joy McDonald, for teaching me what I know about emotions

Bill Herbst, without whose help I could not have launched this project

My children, David, Andrew, Stuart, and Peter Ralston, who encouraged me and stayed out of my way as I worked at the kitchen table

Cherokee Rose, who led the way by believing in her own abilities

Ruth and Bill Bostock, my aunt and uncle, who have loved me unconditionally since the moment I was born

Jill Konrath, my friend and colleague, who guided me to AMA and taught me how to sell

John Macdonald, a friend and mentor who is always there for me at precisely the right moment

Adrienne Hickey, my editor, who saw the value in what I was writing and helped me refine it

Martin Marinaro, who delighted in my progress and success every step of the way

Joanie, Chuck, and Bass Bay Resort, whose nurturing quiet supported me as I wrote

Preface

The heart has its reason which reason knows nothing of.

—Blaise Pascal, French mathematician and philosopher

In my role as a business consultant and psychologist, I am privy to feelings and concerns that are not openly expressed in the work setting. Managers and employees share their fears about pending changes, mistrust of peers, concern about job security, and conflict with bosses and employees.

After twelve years of working in the areas of quality and organizational change, I became discouraged. I saw managers undermine each other, employees hide their opinions, and worthwhile projects fail as hidden agendas and ego needs undermined their success. From this place of frustration, the ideas and concepts in this book were born.

My purpose in writing this book is to get to the heart of the problems we experience at work. I address the unspoken hidden dynamics that keep us silent when we need to talk, "closed" when we need to cooperate, and fearful when we need to trust. This book shows you how honest feelings and opinions are an untapped resource that can contribute to your business success.

Specifically, you will discover the unwritten contract that governs employment relationships, the impact of fear on business decisions, and how hidden agendas work against ideal solutions. The eight principles of emotions described in Chapter 2 will help you address specific work issues such as career dilemmas, environments that make people crazy, problems with employees, and how to succeed with organizational change efforts. The new role of the manager is defined, and action steps are provided to resolve conflicts, develop trust, and open up communication.

This is not a sit-on-the-shelf book but one that is meant to be used. Each chapter includes ideas, principles, case examples, and action exercises to encourage implementation. My hope is that you will enhance your ability to welcome honest feelings, promote individual worth, and see their direct link to business performance. The benefit of these ideas-in-action are organizations that prosper and people who fully contribute their talents.

HIDDEN DYNAMICS

1

Rewriting the Corporate Contract

We are citizens of the world; and the tragedy of our times is that
we do not know this.

—Woodrow Wilson, U.S. President (1913–1921)

Cara: What a day I'm having!

Luke: You look stressed. What's going on?

Cara: It's my boss. He's sending Jordan to the marketing
meeting in Atlanta instead of me.

Luke: What! How can he do that? You've been planning to
go for over a year.

Cara: I know. It makes me want to quit this stupid job. It's
like he doesn't trust me. I guess he thinks Jordan is
better qualified to make the presentation than I am.

Luke: Have you talked to him about it?

Cara: Are you kidding?

This book is about welcoming emotions into the workplace. With
friends, spouses, or lovers, we talk about work a lot. We discuss
what we like, what we don't like, the people we work with, the customers we serve, the situations we encounter, and the company itself—its products, politics, profits, and problems. Yet on the job
itself, only a trusted few know what we really think. For most of us,
our feelings are private.

Welcoming emotions into the workplace is critical to the success of our organizations. The changes now affecting the workplace extend far beyond the particulars of upgrading production and coping with increased market competition. They involve radical shifts in the ways we interact socially and interpersonally. These profound changes cannot be embraced and integrated without addressing our deepest thoughts and feelings. They require us to open our hearts and deal with our emotions.

Taking Down the Walls

In work, as well as in our personal lives, we can no longer succeed without taking down the walls that separate us. Progress demands levels of collaboration and teamwork we never dreamed were possible. Issues such as health care, a global economy, the environment, and balancing the budget cannot be addressed successfully by any one group. From small community and nonprofit organizations to large government agencies, multinational corporations, and entire nations, we are awakening to the blunt fact that we must work together in new ways to solve the problems that face us. Widespread recognition of the need for significant change can be seen in the number of organizations that are restructuring around teams, implementing quality management, and having their people take courses on ways to empower people. We are moving, more by necessity than by choice, from traditional hierarchical structures to leaner, flatter, more fluid organizations. We do so because we possess neither the human nor the financial resources to survive any other way.

The time is past when we can live without one other, pursue independent agendas, permit internal groups be at war, and allow politics to get in the way of our real priorities. Our continued survival depends on our ability to trust each other, share our resources, and build bridges to other people and organizations. We must develop a new perspective.

The Suppression of Emotions

The Unwritten Contract

Why have we tolerated and even encouraged the suppression of candor and emotions in the workplace? Our expectations and behaviors are the result of an unwritten contract between employees and their workplaces that goes something like this:

> The corporation will take care of you for life. In return, you will pledge your loyalty and allegiance—and suppress what you think and feel.

The unspoken rules under the old contract are roughly as follows:

- The organization will provide you with a secure job.
- You will perform as expected and remain loyal to the organization.
- You are to take care of your own personal needs.
- The person you report to determines your future in the company.
- If you disagree with individuals above you, it is best not to say so.

These rules—or some variation on them—are still felt in the vast majority of organizations, whether they are for-profit corporations, nonprofit institutions, or social service agencies. But the rules are hopelessly outdated. They do not acknowledge that organizations can no longer offer us job security and that we cannot continue to hand over the responsibility for our personal well-being to organizations.

Obeying the rules, fitting in, and not expressing who we are is the barter we have made for job security. We bite our tongues in the hopes of protecting our future, but our future is in jeopardy anyway. Organizations can no longer promise job security of any type. For years employers protected workers like family, providing a host of benefits such as fully paid health care, life insurance, pensions, and even savings bonds for children. However, global competition and changing technologies have forced companies to downgrade benefits and shrink existing workforces.

Business as Usual

Despite great technological advancements, the human changes needed for success in the workplace continue to elude us. Managers talk about empowerment, but employees don't believe their words; teams are formed, but they are unable to make anything happen; managers learn new skills, but they quickly return to "business as usual." We are continually reaching for the brass ring, but are unable to grasp it. Denise, a human resources manager for a national retail company recognized for its excellent customer service and quality products, states it well: "We have mastered all the technical aspects of business, but the real challenges are the human ones. Despite our success, people are still unable to reach agreement, work collaboratively, and share resources. We can't get people to trust each other."

To grab the brass ring we must welcome our thoughts and feelings into the workplace. We must foster the courage and provide the safety for people to share their real experience—thoughts, feelings, reactions, and insights. We must create a new sense of community where employees can confront bosses, where business decisions can be questioned, where it is safe to say, "I'm unhappy here," where rocking the boat is expected, where honesty is the norm, and where deep feelings are shared. Honest opinions and authentic feelings are the untapped resources that will help us and our organizations to prosper.

The benefits of addressing and using these feelings are:

- Less stress
- Better understanding of the real issues
- Higher motivation
- More honest relationships
- Improved job performance

Fear of Emotions

Whether we are employees, managers, or executives, we are afraid of emotions. From the time we were babies, we have been taught to suppress our true thoughts and feelings in order to be loved by those around us. In the workplace, we learn to express our positive feelings but not our negative ones. To understand how deeply embedded the idea of not sharing emotions is, try to imagine an executive openly making any of the following statements:

> "I felt left out when I wasn't invited to that meeting."
> "I am really scared about what this change means for me."
> "I feel unappreciated."
> "My feelings were hurt by your actions."
> "I am bored with my job and uninterested in this work."

It is hard to imagine anyone in the workplace—much less an executive—expressing these feelings.

How did we get so far away from allowing feelings—especially negatives ones—to come into the workplace? The answer is simple: We were taught to avoid them. The cultural message is that feelings are too raw and primal and must be channeled into limited and acceptable modes of expression.

We feel an instinctive danger—a pit in the stomach—when we consider sharing our true reactions and feelings. Strong emotions of any kind make us nervous, as do people who are seemingly not in control of themselves. We want them to "get a grip." We are afraid of emotions because we believe they are a force we cannot control. The following are a few of our erroneous assumptions:

- *Emotions are shameful.* We are embarrassed to let others see our strong emotions.
- *Emotions are powerful.* We think we must acquiesce to others when they have strong emotions.
- *Emotions are invalid.* Facts are true but emotions are not to be trusted.
- *Emotions are uncivilized.* We don't know what to do or how to respond to them.

- *Emotions are lies.* We frequently deny what they tell us.
- *Emotions are messy.* We resent the time and energy it takes to deal with them.

Addressing Human and Business Needs

One of the reasons we suppress our emotions at work is because we are prone to either/or thinking about emotions. We believe we must *either* make good business decisions *or* tend to the feelings of people. In our minds, the two options do not go hand in hand. So we either make good business decisions and ignore the human needs, or we address the human needs and neglect the tough business decisions. We have made it an either/or proposition. The truth is that both can be addressed.

To tend to both areas feels a bit like patting our heads and rubbing our stomachs at the same time. We must simultaneously acknowledge the feelings and address the business issues. This is most difficult when our feelings are in conflict with the decisions that need to be made.

Take the case of Allan, a corporate executive who realizes that he must sell off a division of his business. The decision causes Allan great anguish because he values the people working in the division and doesn't want to disrupt their lives. The truth is that Allan must do both: sell the division and help the people through their reactions to the change and into productive new situations. A frequent reaction to this dilemma is to shut down our feelings—and just make the decisions.

Emotions Forced Underground

It is unrealistic to set aside our emotions and feelings in the workplace. Organizational life requires that we work together, side by side, for eight to twelve hours a day, five days a week, fifty weeks a year. We spend more time with our coworkers than we do with our friends, spouses, lovers, or children. Feelings and opinions don't go away just because we walk into the workplace. In the morning we can put on our work clothes, but we cannot take off our emotions.

So what happens to our emotions at work? They go under-ground and become a powerful invisible force. Hours, days, months, sometimes years are spent protecting ourselves from peo-ple we do not trust, avoiding problems we cannot talk about, work-ing around performance issues, faking acceptance of decisions with which we do not agree, putting up with jobs that aren't right for us, or holding back our insights on a situation. Our honest feel-ings remain hidden, denied, choked back—anything to keep them from being felt and expressed—but rarely are they used to help solve our problems.

When I interview individuals about problems in the work-place, a flood of opinions, insights, and feelings comes pouring out. But then those same interviewees say, "Don't tell anyone I said this!" The things that bother us are precisely the things we won't talk about.

There Are No Secrets

When unpleasant emotions are present, we know it. We feel them and react accordingly, regardless of whether they are spoken about openly or held in silently. We have a kind of inner gyroscope that tells us when things are not right. It's a survival instinct. At work, we know when our star is rising, when peers disapprove of us, when we're not in sync with what's going on, when layoffs are coming, which people are likely to get promoted or fired, and when a prospective change might threaten us. We become specula-tive, worried, anxious, and alert during these times. Our emotions are warning us; that is their function.

This awareness is not limited to ourselves. Others can pick up our feelings on their intuitive radar. When we don't like someone or something, others know it. If we acknowledged this uncanny ability, we would realize that all the "private conversations" we have about other people are, on some level, known to them. Fright-ening, isn't it? We spend all this time avoiding difficult issues while we are all dealing with them anyway—only covertly (see Figure 1).

Most of us, however, pretend that we do not have this aware-ness, and instead we get upset stomachs, headaches, and heart-burn. Even those of us who acknowledge these subtle feelings

Figure 1: Hidden dynamics.

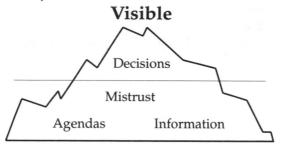

Visible

Decisions

Mistrust

Agendas   Information

Hidden

often do not have the confidence, courage, or certainty to act on them. Our "not so nice" feelings are like a Pandora's box. We've been taught: Don't open the box, don't *ever* open the box. Curiously, however, this is the very box we most need to open. And why not? The box is already open. It is hardly possible to do more harm.

The Vital Need for Emotions

Harvesting Emotional Energy

Our negative feelings and opinions must be harvested for the benefits they bring. They can and should be used to help solve the problems we face. Specifically, they can be used to:

- Improve communications.
- Identify the underlying cause of problems.
- Increase individuals' ability to work as a team.
- Reduce interpersonal conflict.
- Enhance personal performance.
- Gain commitment to new initiatives.

Opening Pandora's Box

When we first open Pandora's box, it can be overwhelming and frightening. Gerry, a new products manager in a software development company, wants to introduce her employees to the new corporate values. But as employees start talking about the values, it becomes painfully clear that they are angry about the way the department is being managed. Many feel isolated and excluded and do not trust each other. Gerry is disappointed. Instead of talking about the new values, the employees are having a gripe session about her lack of leadership! Gerry feels out of control and embarrassed to have these issues discussed publicly, and she doesn't know how to deal with the group's anger. She feels the entire session has taken a wrong turn, derailing her from talking about the new values. What Gerry doesn't realize is that the discussion is not a detour but a direct step toward commitment to the new values.

Gaining acceptance for a new idea often requires the opposite of what we might think. Only after the employees in Gerry's department have addressed their doubts, concerns, and fears are they willing to turn their attention toward the positive aspects of the project. Allowing the expression of bad feelings is like opening the windows of a smoke-filled room to let in the fresh air. Negative energy must be released before positive energy is available.

Emotional Energy as Fuel for Action

Our emotional energy is fuel for action regardless of whether it is created by positive or negative feelings. When we know our feelings and opinions are welcome and feel free to be ourselves, work and work relationships are experienced as vital, energizing, and meaningful. However, when some of our feelings are held back or denied—such as when we think the boss is making a mistake, a peer is out to get us, or a technical problem is being ignored—then it is harder to feel enthusiasm. Emotionally, we have our foot on the brake. By not welcoming unpleasant emotions in our organizations, we are unwittingly smothering the very thing that we desire: emotional commitment and creative involvement. *When negative energy is suppressed, so too is positive energy.*

The Vital Bonds Between Us

Emotions are our human bond with one another. They are what connect us across races, economic barriers, and social differences.

We are connected by the experiences of laughter, tragedy, fear, risk, and joy. The simple experience of laughing together over a joke is a bonding one. Tragedy also bonds us when an employee's family member dies and we rally around him or her to help. And rising to face a challenge bonds us when a risky business venture requires that we team closely and work against unbeatable odds to meet a deadline. We always remember these times. The feelings evoked are what connect us to each other.

At work, we crave the feeling of aliveness that comes from honest relationships, but we do not trust the emotional vulnerability that is necessary to have it. To harvest the vibrant energies of hope, optimism, passion, and enthusiasm, we must also welcome frustration, despair, and fear. Our positive and negative emotions are paired like Siamese twins. If we want the one, we must also embrace the other.

The Need for a New Contract

The relationship between employee and employer must change. Employers must have the flexibility to respond to the marketplace without losing worker commitment and enthusiasm. And employees must feel freer to express genuine needs, concerns, and feelings without fear of retribution. Employees can no longer sit passively and wait for corporations to take care of their futures. Today more than ever, *our work lives affect our personal lives, and our personal lives affect our work lives.*

I remember living by the rules when I discovered unexpectedly that I was pregnant with my fourth child. I sat at my desk, staring at the picture in front of me, realizing that I was pregnant, and worrying about what to do next. Meanwhile, I did not talk to people at work about the fears I felt, the uncertainty in my gut, and my intense need to be supported. I hid my tears and prevented others from seeing the terror inside me—and, as a result, I performed my job halfheartedly.

Should I have sought support at work? Probably. Evidence is mounting that support for personal and home life leads directly to improved performance in the workplace. In a study of 415 diverse businesses and government agencies conducted by the National Employer Supported Child Care Project,* employers reported the following benefits from company policies that promoted the balance between work and home life:

Improved ability to recruit to the company   85 percent
Reduced turnover   65 percent
Reduced absenteeism   53 percent
Increased productivity   49 percent

Workplace as Community

I like to compare the norms and behaviors of our current organizational life to the pioneer farming communities of the nineteenth century and the culture that existed then. Work meant the difference between starvation and having shelter and enough food to eat. There was a profoundly different feeling and attitude about relationships at work.

The barn raising is a wonderful symbol of that time, when family, friends, and neighbors came together to build a barn for a newly wed couple or a family whose barn had burned down or been destroyed. Everyone pitched in, organizing food and sharing the work until the job was done. People participated in each other's lives, and all members of the community contributed. Sometimes they gave help, other times they received help, and somehow it all worked out. The people they worked with were also the people they played with and prayed with. In contrast, much of the isolation we feel today comes from our inability to form supportive communities at work.

In order to create community, we must be able to bring more of who we are, how we feel, and what is happening to us into the workplace. We were never meant to be lonely islands in the sea, impervious to the icy water around us. We are more like the soft-shell clam, which is protected by its shell. But in order to eat and be nourished, the clam must open up its shell and be vulnerable. In

*Sylvia Ann Hewlett, *When the Bough Breaks: The Cost of Neglecting Our Children* (New York: Basic Books, 1991).

order for us to be nurtured, fed, and supported at work, we must shuck our psychological armor and start sharing our needs, feelings, life situations, and vulnerabilities. It is imperative that we build a new kind of workplace—a workplace that accepts our vulnerabilities and our negative and positive opinions and offers us support as we learn to take personal responsibility for our lives.

A Hopeful Vision

In place of traditional job security, we will find safety by transforming our workplaces into communities—communities that encourage and support personal and professional change, respect individual differences, respond to customers, and possess an unwavering commitment to quality products and services. The purpose of the new workplace community is twofold:

1. To respond to the needs of the world and its customers in a brilliant and creative way
2. To foster and support the personal and professional growth of the individuals who serve it

As managers and employees inside these communities, we realize we can no longer find our security in the old way. We stop clinging to expectations of job stability and welcome the opportunity to do what's right, stand up for what we believe, express our needs, and do what needs to be done. We will create our own safety by facing the issues we find and working together to discover the solutions. Our security now must come from trusting what is true and dealing with it openly.

ACTION EXERCISES

Exercise 1: Clarifying Beliefs About Feelings

The purpose of this exercise is to clarify what you believe about emotions. Read each statement and indicate whether you agree or disagree with it. Discuss or reflect on why you feel this way.

1. For most of us, our feelings and honest opinions are private—not shared.
   Agree   Disagree
2. We can no longer succeed in our organization without taking down the walls that separate us from each other.
   Agree   Disagree
3. Honest opinions and authentic feelings are the untapped resource that will help us and our organizations to prosper.
   Agree   Disagree
4. We believe we must either make good business decisions or tend to the feelings of people.
   Agree   Disagree
5. When people have strong feelings and opinions, we intuitively know what they think and feel.
   Agree   Disagree
6. Obeying the rules, fitting in, and giving up who we are is the barter we have made for job security.
   Agree   Disagree
7. It takes too much time and energy to deal with emotions.
   Agree   Disagree

Exercise 2: Recognizing Changes in Business Behaviors and Attitudes

The purpose of this exercise is to recognize the changes in behaviors and attitudes that are occurring in the workplace. Answer and discuss the following questions:

1. How have attitudes and behaviors changed since you started working?

2. What challenges result from these changes?
3. What benefits result from these changes?
4. What are the unspoken and spoken rules about expressing feelings and opinions in your workplace?
5. What current norms about communication would you like to see changed?

Exercise 3: Taking Action to Build Community

The purpose of this exercise is to take actions that build community in the workplace. (Feel free to create your own ideas as well.)

1. Identify three experiences at work where you felt bonded with your coworkers. What created the bond? Was it negative bonding (e.g., we all hated one person) or positive bonding (e.g., we worked on a project or socialized together)?
2. Identify one action you personally can take to create more of a team spirit in your department.
3. Select one person you want to know better and talk to him or her. Discover his or her hobbies and outside interests, and try to understand the issues and challenges the person faces at work.
4. Identify an issue you have withheld your opinion or feelings about. Write down what you wish you could say. Talk about it with someone.
5. List five reasons you don't speak up about an issue you feel strongly about. Keep track and see if the same reasons show up in different situations.
6. Identify two people you find it easy to talk with. List what makes it easy for you to talk to them. Assess how many of these qualities you have.

2

Facts About Feelings

It is not necessary to get away from human nature but to alter its inner attitudes of mind and heart.

—J. F. Newton, minister (1876 –1950)

In the conference room of a large architectural firm, two professionals, Juanita and Noel, are having a conversation over morning coffee.

Juanita: What's gotten into Jeff lately?

Noel: You noticed too?

Juanita: How could I help it? He's been moping around like a wounded puppy dog.

Noel: Yeah, ever since his "promised" promotion fell through.

Juanita: Do you think that's it? I'm not sure what's bugging him. All I know is that his attitude is really sour. Whatever happened, he isn't doing much work these days.

Noel: The worst of it is, he's dampening everyone else's enthusiasm about the upcoming trade show.

Juanita: You're right about that! It's no fun to be around him—he's so cynical—much less try to work with him.

Figure 2. The feelings that we have.

The Impact of Emotions

Juanita and Noel are dealing with emotional issues. They are stymied, not sure what to do, and strongly affected by the dynamics that are occurring in their workplace. All of us have feelings—strong emotions that affect our daily lives—anger, joy, jealousy, greed, love, sadness, hope, and fear (see Figure 2). In the workplace, our emotional needs can manifest themselves as resentments, conflicts, retirements on-the-job, petty turf wars, emotional outbursts, and sabotaging behaviors.

To understand the nature of emotions and how to deal with the feelings in ourselves and others, the following principles are important to keep in mind:

Eight Principles of Emotion

1. Emotional needs express themselves one way or another.
2. Anger is an expression of need.
3. Our feelings and needs are not wrong or bad.
4. Emotions are the gateway to vitality and feeling alive.
5. We can address emotional issues and still save face.
6. Immediate reactions to problems often disguise deeper feelings.
7. We must clarify individual needs before problem solving with others.
8. We need to express positive feelings and communicate negative ones.

Principle 1: *Emotional Needs Express Themselves One Way or Another*

To better understand our primal emotions and the dynamics at play, we can learn from the extreme of violence in the workplace. Strong emotional reactions are the result of long-standing, frustrated needs. Violence can occur when emotions spill over. Sexual harassment and illicit affairs are grounded in unmet needs and emotional suppression. At these two edges, we can see how desperate we become when our human needs are denied.

While the majority of corporate workers handle the routine human indignities that come with employment, a tiny percentage crack under the strain. Newspapers report increasing incidence of violence in the workplace, which was virtually unheard of in the late 1980s. Since that time, acts of violence have increased. "One hundred people were murdered in 1993, which is up from seventy individuals the previous year," according to authority Joseph Kinney, executive director of the National Safe Workplace Institute in Chicago.

Emotional tensions and fears can go underground and then erupt in violence. Take the case of a Native American friend of mine who spent nineteen years in prison for murder. Today, this man is a gentle marathon runner, artist, philosopher, and spiritual teacher. One night we talked about the brutal murder he had committed. It had been an incredible high for him. He told me, "I have never felt so powerful! The day after I felt exhilarated—like no one could touch me—like I would never die—like I was God. It was only later that the feelings of grief and sadness came."

All his life he had been the underdog. As a Native American with little formal education and no money, he was frequently treated with disdain. He desperately wanted to *be somebody*. He wanted to feel important. And in the act of murdering another human being, he felt powerful. The only way he could get this feeling was to murder a stranger in cold blood. Our human need to feel valuable and important cannot be denied. In the extremes, this need can express itself constructively in courageous acts or destructively in violent acts. One way or another, our need to feel important expresses itself.

Principle 2:   Anger Is an Expression of Need

Individuals who commit violent crimes are angry. I have learned much about emotions from Elleva Joy McDonald, with whom I have talked about the problems caused by the rejection of anger. Elleva Joy McDonald is a bodywork therapist who works with emotional issues. In one of our conversations, she said to me,

> We don't *like* anger—we don't accept it. We really don't know what to do with it, in ourselves or others. We think all anger is fundamentally bad. But there are two kinds of anger. One kind of anger is good. We need it to survive. It's the anger that comes from our dignity, rising up and shouting,"No, I won't let you treat me like this! This is not right! I won't tolerate this anymore!" It's the part of us that propels us into action.

We need this first type of anger. Without it we are wimps, unable to rally to our own defenses, strike out in new directions, and put an end to manipulative, abusive situations. It is necessary for survival—for our lives to be our own. *But we are terrified of it.* This is the anger we must learn to accept.

The second kind of anger is not healthy. It is utterly hopeless and despairing. At its core is the bitterness and rage that come from the loss of hope. This is the anger that causes people to kill—themselves as well as others—when they feel, "There are no options left. Someone must pay. Something must happen. If I go down, you go down! Nothing is possible. Nothing is ever going to change. It's hopeless. I can't bear it any longer."

But our anger does not have to be vented in self-destructive ways. It can be used to help us discover our real needs if we recognize and address the vulnerabilities that cause the anger.

Principle 3:   Our Feelings and Needs Are Not Wrong or Bad

The murder my friend committed was wrong. But his underlying needs and feelings were not wrong! His need was a human need that we all have: *the need to feel important.* Our feelings are not wrong or bad. When we accept our feelings, we accept ourselves. Our feelings tell us what we want and need. Fear can tell us we need to be reassured; mistrust can tell us we need to talk to somebody; dislike can tell us we desire a change. When we deny these feelings, we deny our needs—and depression, despair, and even violence can be the result.

When acts of violence occur, it is not only the violent person who is responsible and needs help. We must begin to understand how others and the organizational culture are also involved. Where was the employee's manager when he or she felt so discouraged? What happened when the early alarms went off? Why did everyone turn away and pretend not to see? Why didn't someone respond to the cries for help? How often did the work culture suppress the expression of sadness, anger, and even minor frustration? How much did the harsh expectation that "everyone is responsible for his or her own problems" cause people to focus on work at human expense?

Principle 4: Emotions Are the Gateway to Vitality and Feeling Alive

Unmet emotional needs are linked not only with violent behavior but also with inappropriate sexual behavior. Our sexual drives express pent-up emotional needs. When these needs go unmet, they can show up in inappropriate sexual conduct.

A high-ranking executive of a large organization is in the process of a divorce. He feels a tremendous loss. Meanwhile, the business pressures on him are enormous. He desperately needs emotional support, but he denies this need and the loneliness he feels at the top. With support no longer available at home, he looks elsewhere. He turns more and more to his administrative assistant—a married woman—for emotional support. She accompanies him on business trips. They have an affair. The situation causes enormous frustration in the organization because the woman influences his decisions. There is lot of office talk and resentment. His behaviors are detrimental, not only to himself but to the organization.

In a different situation, an attractive woman manager uses flirtation, innuendo, and risqué body language to influence her male superiors. Inside she feels insecure, but she covers these feelings with suggestive sexual behavior. In the short term, she gets the attention she wants and maybe even the job assignments. But inside she feels undeserving of her success and even more inadequate and anxious.

Our sexual needs become exaggerated when we work day and night in long meetings using only our brains and don't acknowledge our need for laughter, movement, emotion, and variety. We create a volatile situation. Then we eat too much, drink too much, or misuse our sexual energy. It isn't just sex we want. We want to feel *alive*. We want the safety of belonging and the warmth of intimacy.

To engage with work fully, we need to access the feelings of hope and optimism, excitement and interest, and promote feelings of appreciation and support. It is our feelings that determine whether we look forward to daily activities or want to do something different, whether we contribute our best or simply meet the basic requirements. Motivation and enthusiasm, inspiration and hope cannot be attained without tapping emotional energy. Emotions are the gateway to vitality and connection.

Principle 5: We Can Address Emotional Issues and Still Save Face

Dwight, a customer service manager in an engineering firm, calls the company's employee assistance counselor for help. He wants to fire Brad, a young employee, because of inappropriate behavior. At first Brad made explicit sexual remarks to female coworkers, but after one warning from Dwight, he stopped. Several weeks later, however, he started to be sexually aggressive with a male coworker. Dwight feels this behavior is clearly unacceptable in the working world.

Dwight wants advice about how to fire Brad without repercussion. Also, he is afraid. Brad has made several comments about owning a gun and wanting "to blast some people away." Dwight's initial plans for firing Brad are to hold a closed-door meeting, terminate him in the presence of three managers, have a police escort show him to the door, give him a box with the contents of his desk, and send him on his way!

Dwight and the counselor talk for a long time before settling on what to do. Brad clearly has a problem—a problem that is being acted out sexually. At some point in his life, he may have been sexually abused. The abuse issues may be rising to the surface and revealing themselves in inappropriate behavior. His actions are a cry for help.

It is not right for Dwight to ignore Brad's behavior—that would be the worst thing to do. But neither does he need to humiliate Brad. Dwight chooses to fire Brad in a way that leaves his dignity intact. Brad is an excellent contributor and a hard worker, and Dwight tells him this. But he has a problem that he, Dwight, and the organization cannot ignore. Brad is terminated and referred to a sexual abuse clinic. Dwight stays in touch with Brad for several months to support his progress and job change. No violence results from the situation.

We do not want volatile or extreme emotions breaking out in the workplace. We know that without limits, boundaries, and expectations about emotional control, relationships and work suffer. Social norms about behaviors exist for a reason. Our expectations of emotional control help us to:

- Reduce volatile reactions.
- Create an environment of safety.
- Provide the balance necessary for our well-being.
- Ensure the stability of the group.
- Focus on tasks that need to be done.

However, completely suppressing our feelings keeps us from being sensitive to:

- Dealing with work situations that are abusive to our well-being
- Knowing our larger goals and dreams
- Seeing important clues in interactions with others
- Recognizing unhealthy motives and con games
- Appreciating our need for balance and connection

If welcomed and used properly, our emotions can lead us out of destructive work relationships and situations into clear realities that support who we are and what we need.

Principle 6:   Immediate Reactions to Problems Often Disguise Deeper Feelings

Our initial emotional response to a problem is often not the same as the deeper feelings involved. Donna, a health care consultant, walks into her office one day and discovers the contents of her desk piled in the corner. As she surveys the situation, she becomes angry. She thinks, "Who would dump my stuff on the floor without asking me first? This is an insult. Someone is going to hear about this." Shortly, Donna's supervisor comes in and says, "An emergency came up and we have to use your office for two weeks. I'm sorry we have to move you unexpectedly. I didn't have a chance to warn you so I put your things together in the corner so you could move them easily." Later that night Donna reflects on the incident and realizes that although her initial reactions were anger and indignation, her real feelings are being hurt and even a little afraid that perhaps she's not really wanted in her job.

We have four possible responses to the presence of strong emotions. Three responses are to run away, get angry, or deny the importance and intensity of what we are really feeling. The fourth option is to identify our real feelings correctly and use them to address the situation by sharing our concerns and asking for what we need. It takes courage to implement this option. Let's look at the possible reactions to strong emotions in Figure 3.

Running Away

A frequent response to intense feelings is to remove ourselves from the situation by avoiding others, not talking to them, acting like they are not in the room, pretending the event never occurred, or even moving to a new location or job. When a situation or person activates our deepest emotions, we may go to great lengths to avoid these feelings. At work, we avoid facing our bosses, making presentations, working with specific individuals, tackling a techni-

Figure 3. Reactions to strong emotions.

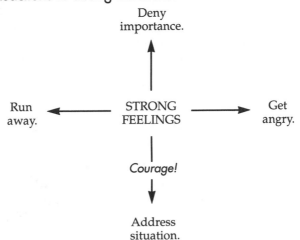

cal problem, attending certain meetings, or ignoring topics we need to discuss—all in an attempt to avoid the feelings that are activated by a situation.

Getting Angry

Anger, although it appears direct, is one of the strongest avoidance tactics we have because it keeps us away from our deeper, more vulnerable emotions. Outwardly, we seethe with resentment, yell at someone, stomp up and down, slam doors, make sarcastic remarks, talk behind the person's back, or sabotage his or her success—all because we don't want to feel the emotions that are being activated inside of us. Anger frequently masks feelings of being hurt. It is safer to react with the brittle, harsh emotions of anger and resentment rather than express the deeper, more vulnerable feelings of hurt, disappointment, and sadness.

Denying Importance

When a person or situation hurts us in a significant way, we may attempt to diminish our strong feelings by rationalizing, "This isn't really that important. I'm a 'big girl/boy.' This will blow over. I'll get used to it. They really didn't mean it." Sometimes, we are able to forget about the incident and go about our business. But if the situation really bothers us, lingering resentment remains and small incidents remind us of the very feelings we are trying to forget.

Addressing the Situation

Identifying our real feelings and then addressing the situation is the best—but possibly most difficult—way to respond. But first we must figure out what we're feeling. When strong emotions are present, it is not unusual for us initially to experience all three of the other possible reactions—running away, getting angry, and denying importance—to the situation. I remember observing my own irrational responses to a friend's neglect. Initially I pretended I didn't care and wasn't bothered by her behavior. But I am not a great pretender and was only able to sustain my indifference for a day. The next day when I thought about the situation, I felt angry and resentful and imagined myself lecturing, moralizing, and delivering ultimatums about how I should be treated better. Later that day, I entertained vivid fantasies of my friend leaving town so I would never have to feel this way again. In a short period of forty-eight hours, I watched myself experience all three reactions to the feelings of hurt and insecurity.

To make the best use of primal emotions, we must move beyond our initial reactions and claim our feelings before addressing the situation and engaging in problem solving with others. Until then, our actions, problem solving, and solutions are aimed at the wrong problem. In the earlier example, Donna could have easily responded by asserting her right to be treated differently or by pretending the incident did not bother her. However, Donna decides to address her real feelings and so she takes a different approach. She sets up a meeting with her manager and asks for feedback on her performance. She expresses her need to be assured about the value of her work. Explicitly addressing the need to feel valued is more beneficial to Donna than discussing the contents of her desk on the floor!

Solutions based on surface reactions never satisfy us because they do not respond to the heart of our concern. Many a lawsuit

has been fought because of deep hurt activated by the way someone is treating us. But even when we win and there is financial re-
muneration, there is still the feeling of not quite getting what we
wanted. True satisfaction comes when we identify, accept, and respond to our deeper needs.

Principle 7: We Must Clarify Individual Needs Before Problem Solving With Others

It is a myth that we will ever become "mature enough" or "important enough" to stop having needs or caring if others like us. No
amount of status and income can replace the joy and connection
that we feel when successfully bonding with and being appreciated
by others. But to get this approval and keep it, we deny our feelings and do not admit them to ourselves—much less other people.

To identify our real needs and claim them, we must allow our
reactions and feelings to exist and not judge them. Knowing we do
not have to act on our feelings, express them to anyone, or fix the
situation frees us to be absolutely honest with ourselves.

In a seminar on self-empowerment, participants are asked to
identify a problem in their work life. Next, they are told to write ten
or more statements describing how they really feel about the problem. They are told not to share these feelings with anyone because
it might inhibit what they write. After participants complete the
task, they describe how it felt to write "unedited" statements. They
make the following comments:

> "I feel guilty for having these thoughts."
> "I have never expressed these feelings before."
> "I hope no one sees this paper!"
> "I learned something new by doing this."
> "If I admit how I feel, I have to fix it."

The following statements block the expression of feelings in
yourself and others. Read them and note which ones you use
most frequently in your internal dialogue or in conversations
with others.

Communication Blocks

"Why don't I [you] just forget about this."
"This is nothing compared to what someone else is dealing with."
"If I [you] hadn't messed up, this wouldn't be happening."
"Didn't I say this wouldn't work out?"
"It will all be better tomorrow."
"I [you] must fix this situation."
"I [you] must be a bad person."

Too often, these are the statements we make instead of simply accepting the feelings of ourselves and others.

Principle 8:   We Need to Express Positive Feelings and Communicate Negative Ones

The first challenge in using our emotional energy at work is to acknowledge the feelings we experience. But merely understanding our feelings is not sufficient. The second step is to learn to express them in such a way that they can be heard.

For some, acknowledging emotions means relearning spontaneity and a childlike sense of wonder, getting out of our rational minds, and allowing our feelings to blossom. Too many of us are overly analytical, and have lost our emotional spontaneity as we have become immersed in structures of rationality and logic. Yet others of us are too wanton and free with the expression of our emotions and lack the discipline to discuss difficult issues with cool intention and the necessary degree of rationality.

For expressive individuals, becoming sensitive to our emotions means learning to separate ourselves from negative feelings, detach, and observe, instead of responding to every emotional cue. It means learning to redirect hot emotional reactions into calm communication and the ability to listen to each other instead of taking things personally.

Once feelings are identified, they must be communicated so others can hear them. If our purpose is to inflict guilt or seek revenge, we are not ready to talk constructively. It is important to express feelings so they can be heard. Positive feelings can be expressed spontaneously. When we express positive feelings, we affirm our aliveness, enthusiasm, and responsiveness as human beings.

As my consultant friend Bill Herbst says, "Some of us have too many words in our heads and we miss the music. Others of us have too few words in our heads and fail to logically interpret or communicate our meaning."

As much as we like to feel good and share positive feelings, it is impossible to have long-term working relationships without experiencing negative feelings. Differences of opinion and conflicting needs are part of working closely with other people. When negative emotions are not communicated, they grow larger and more intense. Negative emotions are like ferocious pit bulls: The longer they exist without being acknowledged, the more they work up a frenzy internally. Anger denied turns eventually into rage, suspicions repressed dissolve into mistrust and blame, dislike ignored festers into cold hatred. We must communicate strong, negative emotions in ways that allow others to feel safe and not under assault. Anger carries with it blame and causes us to erect defenses or to retaliate to protect our integrity.

The key to communicating negative emotions is *careful communication* rather than direct expression. If I am angry about how you are behaving, I can either throw my anger at you or carefully communicate what I am feeling. Impulsive, unfocused expression of my feelings is a shock that will probably send you away.

The Value of Listening and Communicating

Ironically, listening to the other person is the key to communicating our own needs. When we listen well, we help the other person get clear on his or her feelings and needs. We also create a receptive environment for our needs to be discussed. Listening helps us to:

- Understand the situation better.
- Identify what the other person needs.
- Determine what we can do.

- Increase our ability to respond creatively.
- Stop defending our position.
- Gain cooperation from the other person.

Too often we try to problem solve with another person without understanding the real issues. To communicate a problem to another person, follow these action steps:

1. Affirm the importance of your working relationship. Say, "I would like to talk with you about an issue that concerns me. But first I want you to know how important you are to me and how much I value our working relationship." Be specific about what you value.

2. Share your feelings. Say "The other day, when _____ happened, I felt_____." Be specific about the event, and describe your reactions and feelings.

3. Ask the other person to share his or her point of view and feelings. Carefully listen to the point of view, understand it, and summarize his or her views.

4. Ask for what you need. Be specific. Say, "What I want [need/would like] to happen is _____." Then listen and summarize the other person's response.

5. Mutually agree on what actions you will both take.

As we accurately communicate our feelings about difficult issues and let others know that something is amiss in the relationship, we alert the group or individual that a course correction is needed if we are to remain effective teammates and coworkers, thus protecting the path toward real productivity.

The Need to Be Involved

All too often, managers relegate the task of dealing with emotional issues to the human resources specialists, who become a crutch that allows managers to wash their hands of the situation. But the offices of the experts are too far away, the wait is too long, the response is too brief, and the need is too great to leave emotional issues solely to the human resources professionals.

Managers and employees alike must become knowledgeable in human emotions. We must learn new ways to relate to each other that include listening and caring and the ability to set limits and say no. Understanding our own emotions is the best teacher. If we honor the feelings and needs in ourselves, we will then honor them in others.

As we understand the essence of emotions, we see that our emotions are like the elements of nature—sometimes raw, violent, changing, and unpredictable; other times pleasant, warm, inviting, and steady. Whether warm or cold, violent or steady—our emotions can be controlled but never completely tamed. And just as too much contact with the raw elements of nature is dangerous for us, neither is it good for us to completely succumb to our feelings. Similar to our need for contact with nature, we need to be in touch with our emotions on a regular basis, but not completely at their mercy.

As we begin to deal with emotions, we realize just how much they affect our business every day. Team effectiveness is strengthened or weakened by the existence of trust and teamwork. Our ability to implement change is highly dependent on emotional buy-in and commitment. The relationship between managers and employees determines whether we feel empowered or negated. And our ability to contribute our best talent is affected by whether we feel safe from pending layoff and whether others recognize our skills. Success at work is often determined by whether we deal with these issues or not.

ACTION EXERCISES

Exercise 1: Clarifying Your Real Feelings

The purpose of this exercise is to clarify your real feelings about a problem you are facing.

1. Identify the most difficult problem you face right now at work and write it in the center of the circle. Around the circle, write true statements about what you think, feel, want, dislike, hope, and like about this situation. Include contradictory feelings and emotions. Do not edit your responses.

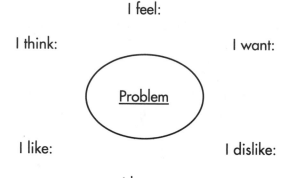

2. When you are done, write one sentence that states what you really want and need.

Exercise 2: Discovering What Others See When You're Upset

The purpose of this exercise is to determine what behaviors we exhibit when we're upset. Our behavior tells others that we are upset. When we encounter a problem, we have typical ways of reacting that communicate our discomfort.

1. Ask coworkers these questions to identify how you communicate when you are upset:

   • When have you seen me upset?

- How do I frequently act when I am upset? Minor upsets? Major upsets?
- Specifically, what behaviors tell you that I am unhappy, angry, or dissatisfied?
- What types of situations seem to upset me the most?

2. After you have secured this information, summarize your behavior and identify any changes you want to make. List:

- The things that upset you the most
- The behaviors that indicate you are upset
- The specific changes you want to make

Exercise 3: Becoming Aware of Your Beliefs About Anger

The purpose of this exercise is to help you become aware of your attitudes and beliefs about anger.

1. Read each sentence stem and quickly write up to five statements that complete it. Write the first thoughts that comes to your mind. Don't think too much!

- When I am angry, I . . . [feel, wish, do]
- When I am angry, I wish others would . . . [do, say, help by]
- When others are angry, I . . . [do, wish, avoid, react by]
- Violence makes me want to . . . [feel, do, think]
- Anger is basically . . .

2. Read what you have written and answer these questions:

- What are your basic attitudes and beliefs about anger?
- How do you typically respond to anger in yourself and others?
- How do these beliefs and attitudes affect your work relationships?

Exercise 4: Learning to Listen

The purpose of this exercise is to listen to another person's point of view. Practice good listening before a crisis arises so you can listen when you are in a difficult situation. The following are a sample of listening responses. Use them, but don't overuse them, to enhance your listening skills.

- "I understand."
- "You feel sad" (angry, hurt, etc.).
- "You are not sure what to do."
- "You are worried about this."
- "This isn't easy for you."
- "I hear you."

1. Practice listening skills by selecting someone and giving him or her your complete attention for fifteen minutes. Don't ask any questions. Use some of the listening responses above. Avoid repetition of the same phrase.

2. At the end of fifteen minutes, ask the person how it felt to have you listen to them.

3. Now ask yourself these questions:

- Did you want to jump in?
- How did it feel to only listen?
- What were the benefits to you? To the other person?
- Where can you use listening more in real work situations?

3

Don't Rock the Boat

Anyone who has begun to think places some portion of the world in jeopardy.

—John Dewey, U.S. philosopher and educator

It is 1986. The space shuttle *Challenger* is scheduled to take off on a visible mission. For the first time ever a civilian has been chosen in a national competition to be one of the flight crew. Reporters interview Christa McAuliffe, the first "teacher in space," and television shows broadcast endless footage of her classroom and family. The public's interest has been captured, and expectations are high.

But all is not well at the Cape. The weather is not cooperating—it is cold and there is ice on the launch pad—and a mysterious technical problem repeatedly delays the carefully timed lift-off. Engineers and technical personnel work day and night on the problem of the "O-rings"—the rubber seals in the rocket booster joints—which is serious, even potentially deadly. Tension rules, and tempers run short. Should the mission be scrapped?

A teleconference is held to make a decision. Two engineers report that they have not been able to solve the O-ring problem. Heated discussion and debate follow about whether to proceed with or cancel the scheduled lift-off. There is a fundamental conflict of opinion. Management wants to launch, lobbying that the technical problem is not that serious and postponement would dampen public interest. Engineering holds out for a no-go decision, saying the O-rings are no small issue. The weather is a factor in how well they will hold, and it has never been this cold for a launch before.

A final vote is called. A senior vice president turns to the head of engineering and says, "Take off your engineering hat and put on your management hat!" The two presenting engineers are not permitted to vote because of their lower rank. Ballots are tallied, and the decision is unanimous in favor of lift-off.

All systems are go. The countdown resumes, and in the morning *Challenger* lifts off. For a moment, everything seems fine. One of the engineers turns to the other and says, "Thank you God, we missed that bullet!"

Barely seconds later, the *Challenger* explodes into a massive, smoke-enveloped fireball. Everyone watches in horror. Cameras track the unspeakable nightmare as the ship and its booster rockets disintegrate, and debris falls out of the sky toward the ocean below. The *Challenger* and its crew have ceased to exist.

The Pressure to Conform

There is much to learn from the *Challenger* disaster. In one shocking event, we see with clarity the all-too-human dynamics at work inside our organizations. Conformity to peer pressure is a powerful force. In that fateful meeting, the head of engineering caved in to the majority opinion instead of holding out for what he knew was right.

Conformity occurs *when we give up what we know is right in order to fit in with the group.* It is often difficult to stand up for what we know is unacceptable behavior. We do not get extra points for being the "organizational irritant." Mavericks are exalted in the movies, but in real life, they are thrown out, barely tolerated, or at best treated as a mixed blessing. Such individuals are shunted away from power. It's one thing to root for a fictional character who bucks the system; it's quite another to risk the livelihood you need to feed your family and buy the kids' shoes. We conform not because we are weak but because everything we have is at stake. Yet our ready conformity to the majority leaves us with lackluster and sometimes disastrous decisions.

Fear in the Workplace

Underlying conformity is fear, a pervasive emotion in organizations today. We are afraid to confront authority, afraid of reprisal, afraid of being vulnerable, afraid of appearing ineffective or powerless, afraid of not being accepted, afraid of alienating others, afraid of looking stupid, afraid of losing control—the list of fears is endless. We must realize the level of conscious and subconscious fear that exists in our organizations. Fear cannot be underestimated.

Think about the statements that are common in our workplaces and the messages they send:

"Do what you're told."
"Don't rock the boat."
"Take care of number one."
"Be a team player. Fit in."

We send these messages to each other both overtly and covertly. The underlying directive is don't make waves, take care of yourself, and obey the rules. What we get for our efforts are watered-down decisions and poor compromises. In our organizations, it's the good news that travels up, while bad news sinks like a stone. Managers have trouble obtaining the information they need because employees are hesitant and afraid to communicate bad news. And some managers simply do not want to hear anything but positive reports.

Fear at the Top

Fear exists at all levels. Take the case of Nathan, a top executive in an insurance company.

Nathan links the success of his career to an innovative product designed to respond to rising health care costs. But results are disappointing after three years of intensive investment in product development, new staff, sales training, and promotional activities. Profits are foundering and customer complaints are mounting. The new product is in trouble. In desperation, Nathan hires a team of outside consultants to identify the problems and recommend solutions.

The consultants discover significant barriers to success. Customers want customized product options that are labor-intensive to deliver. The computer system needs significant upgrading to handle customized options. In addition, to sell the product, sales professionals need in-depth knowledge of competitors, familiarity with product options, and strong partnerships with the customers. Internal resistance to the new product is strong because the core business is based on high-volume, standardized insurance products, rather than a customized medical product. Early on, many of these issues had been identified by the sales force, but the home office did not have the reputation of listening or responding to input from the field. Therefore, this information was kept inside the sales force.

Upon seeing the consultants' report, Nathan becomes livid. He tells each person on his staff, "This is the worst report I've ever seen." Then he asks, "Do you agree with the report?" Of course, they say no. Nathan fires the manager of the product area, dismisses the consultants, and discredits their findings as ludicrous. Nathan is afraid. He is afraid of failure—the flip side of his equally strong need for success. His fears make it impossible for him to hear the information. The data is too threatening.

Any manager or employee who dares to contradict Nathan is in imminent danger of losing a job. Make no mistake about it—this is not an environment where anyone is likely to be candid with management.

Whenever this level of resistance occurs, there is always fear underneath. When we are afraid, we cannot hear others' points of view. Bad news carries an implicit judgment that is threatening to us. If something we care about is "bad," we think we are bad! These are the wages of fear—and no one is immune. Our fears cause us to blow up, become suspicious, talk behind people's backs, blame others, sneak around, and defend ourselves against shadows. Executives are every bit as likely to encounter immobilizing fear as mail room trainees.

Fear of Authority

Most of us are afraid to confront our boss because of decades of cultural conditioning. We are taught by word and deed not to challenge people at higher levels or people with more power and prestige. The very fiber of our work culture is built around agreeing with the person in charge—even if that person is wrong.

In a consumer products group, the top-level managers invite people to "speak with more candor." Among the employees, there is discussion about what this statement "really means" and great skepticism about whether anyone will respond to this request. The unanimous feeling among the employees is, "I think *not!*"

A single invitation by management for candor cannot undo decades of programming to the contrary. Employees are afraid to challenge their bosses, and bosses often do not know how to respond when employees do. Despite open-door policies, there are a multitude of problems that employees will never tell their managers. If managers want information, they must *actively solicit it from employees.* They must go out and dig for it, or they will not know what's really happening. Managers must create an environment where employees feel safe to share information, or all the digging in the world will turn up nothing.

Fear of Confrontation

Speaking honestly to peers about interpersonal and performance issues is scary. I have seen managers literally get sick to their stomachs with fear before going into a team-building session where they are planning to discuss the issues they have with each other. It is hard for us to confront problems such as unmet expectations, personality conflicts, perceived betrayals, lack of trust, and differences in our wants and needs. We learn early in life to avoid problems in relationships. By the time we are adults, we are adept at ignoring what bothers us. But good working relationships require that we talk openly with bosses, peers, and employees about what we want and need and whether or not we are getting it.

Fear of Conflict

One particularly vivid example of conflict avoidance took place between Roger, the president of a retail business, and one of his managers, Dave.

Roger's company starts small but grows considerably over the years. As it expands, a human resources/administrative function is required. Roger promotes Dave from sales manager into the newly created position, even though Dave does not have any background or experience in human resources or administration.

Soon after the decision is made, Roger knows that he has made a mistake. But he doesn't want to hurt Dave's feelings, so he avoids the issue. For six years the organization works around the fact that Dave is an inadequate administrator. No one is happy about the situation. Eventually, the need for effective administration of the business becomes too big to ignore.

Faced with this reality, Roger knows he has to take action. He develops a plan. He asks his staff to go through career assessment testing to identify their strengths and weaknesses. Next, he calls a meeting of managers to discuss the results of the assessment. Throughout the meeting, Roger covertly uses peer feedback and the assessment information to remove Dave from his administrative job. Under the guise of a feedback session, Roger "restructures" the job away from Dave. Not once does Roger talk to Dave about his lack of skill, nor does Roger discuss with Dave ahead of time the restructuring he has in mind. During the meeting, Roger avoids any direct responsibility for the change, stating that the decision is based on peer feedback.

As a businessman, Roger has the reputation of "leaping tall buildings in a single bound." Yet he cannot tell Dave that he is not getting the job done or take responsibility for the change that has to be made. He wants to be "nice." He tries everything—everything but telling the truth.

After the meeting, no one feels good about what has taken place. The other managers feel guilty for giving feedback to a peer that causes his removal and humiliation. Each of them thinks, "If Roger can do this to Dave, he can do it to me next." The result is a complete breakdown of trust.

When fear is present, we:

- Hesitate to share our ideas.
- Resist change and unexpected requirements.
- Follow the rules and procedures to feel safe.
- View feedback as criticism.
- Look out for ourselves and our backsides.
- Do not voice our objections and concerns.

When we feel safe in our relationships—accepted for who we are and supported in our efforts—and know that there will be no negative repercussions for our honesty, we are able to:

- Contribute our ideas freely.
- Explore innovative solutions to problems.
- Listen and respond when others tell us we have made a mistake.
- Speak up when we disagree.
- Help others when they need it.
- Learn and adapt to change faster.

How to Reduce Fear

The following are specific ways to help reduce fear in the workplace:

- *Acknowledge the presence of fear.* Fear has a lot of power because we don't acknowledge its existence. It's not cool to say we are afraid. When fear might be present, comment on it by saying:

  "What are you concerned about?"
  "What fears do we have about this?"
  "It can be frightening to change."
- *Encourage questions and input.* While direct communication is ideal, it is not always realistic. Structure innovative ways for employees to voice their concerns and questions. Encourage anonymous notes or talking to a specified person who will communicate with the person in charge.
- *Invite "dumb" questions.* Encourage people to ask dumb

questions by saying, "Now I want you to ask a question that you think everyone in the room but you knows the answer to."

• *Identify what contributes to fear, and change it.* Discover beliefs, attitudes, and assumptions that keep employees from expressing their opinions and feelings. Ask these questions:

"What encourages you to express your ideas openly?"
"What hinders you from expressing your ideas openly?"
"What changes are needed to reduce fear?"

Why Are We Afraid?

At the heart of it all lies our need for acceptance as human beings. On the surface we may call the problem lack of leadership, poor morale, racial discrimination, inadequate teamwork, or low trust. But always at the center lies our need to be valued as human beings. The rest of it—our conflict-ridden behaviors—come from the deep fears we have about not feeling accepted or appreciated.

When our need for acceptance is not met, we become afraid, our defenses are activated, and we react. Our need for acceptance is like a pebble that gets tossed into a pond. When the pebble drops, it very quickly disappears from sight, and all we can see are the waves that ripple out. See Figure 4.

Figure 4. The ripple effect of fear, anger, and conflict.

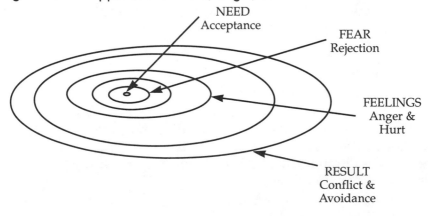

Fear is the first ripple, and the waves of anger and conflict expand from there. The results that ripple out from fear are lawsuits, turf wars, lack of cooperation, and interpersonal conflicts. To get to the bottom of it all, we must go for the pebble. And we must know that it is the pebble of acceptance that we are looking for and not get distracted and confused by all the waves. To reduce fear, we must respond to three specific needs:

1. The need to be liked
2. The need to be appreciated
3. The need to belong

The Need to Be Liked

The need to be liked is a powerful motive. We instinctively realize the importance of being liked. It helps us get things done, be promoted, win projects, influence others, and gain recognition. Not being liked causes us to have difficulty with peers, get passed over for promotions, lose future opportunities, fail to gain cooperation, and suffer a bad reputation.

No matter how much we pretend, no one truly *wants* to be disliked. The hardest, toughest people are often the most tender inside. One manager said to me, "I act like a bear and people are afraid of me, but inside I'm a wuss."

The fact that we want to be liked, to feel safe, and to be appreciated often results in the formation of cliques. Workplaces are reminiscent of high school when it comes to cliques. We have old-timer cliques, technical cliques, minority cliques, smoker cliques, old-boy cliques, manager cliques, employee cliques, and front-room and back-room cliques.

Cliques are normal. They are the natural grouping of people who share an experience or interest in common. Cliques create a sense of belonging, but they also leave people out. It's the simple exclusions that cause bad feelings: not being invited to lunch, hearing conversations change when you approach, not being asked to participate. There are also status symbols associated with being in different cliques: higher walls, no time cards, better equipment, more support. The "have nots" are often resentful and envious of the more privileged "haves."

Most employees don't want to work in a clique environment. They say:

"There are too many cliques here."
"I want to learn about what goes on in other areas."
"I feel cut off from other groups and departments."
"I want to be treated with more respect."
"I want to feel like we are all in this together."

The Need to Be Appreciated

Many negative situations can be repaired by recognizing and appreciating individual differences and contributions. Here is one example.

A welfare agency is on the verge of a costly lawsuit with an angry employee, Thongsoy. Jim, his manager, is at a loss. In a last-ditch effort to salvage the situation before the lawyers and courts close in, Jim talks with the human resources manager. How did the situation get so out of hand? What can he do?

Thongsoy is from Laos. Jim has little experience managing people with backgrounds other than his. He tends to stick with what is comfortable and familiar to him. Unconsciously, he gives his friends most of the special assignments. After three years of watching this pattern, Thongsoy becomes discouraged and angry. He wants to grow and eventually be promoted, but he sees little hope of getting help from Jim.

Things finally come to a head when Thongsoy is given a long overdue performance review. Jim tells Thongsoy that he is not successfully completing the tasks in his current job. This is the last straw. Thongsoy threatens a lawsuit.

After the human resources manager interviews other employees and spends time talking with Thongsoy and Jim, the problem becomes clear. Jim feels intimidated and annoyed by Thongsoy. Thongsoy's English is difficult for Jim to understand, and he cannot relate to Thongsoy's interests or background. Because their communication is superficial, Jim is confused by Thongsoy's suggestions and requests.

The first step to fix this near disaster is to have Jim spend time with Thongsoy, talk to him, learn about his background, identify his skills, and see how he works. Repairing their relationship is not a straightforward or easy process—especially given their history.

As Jim gradually comes to know Thongsoy better, his recognition and appreciation of Thongsoy grows, as well as his ability to use his talents appropriately. Thongsoy is able to ask Jim for the help he needs and starts to feel that he is appreciated and his ideas and suggestions are valued. The feelings and perceptions of both change as they learn to work together, and a costly lawsuit is avoided.

The Need to Belong

We need to feel that we belong in order to contribute our best. Too often, we fail miserably at bonding and connecting with each other. Even in meetings where we don't know each other, little time is spent on introductions or finding common ground. Instead, we dive right into the work, ignoring the fact that we don't even know the name of the person sitting next to us.

Our lack of attention to the need to belong is evident in the way we treat new employees. Many describe their first day on the job like this:

> "Well, they took me to my desk, showed me my phone, and that was it. From there on out I was on my own."
> "I showed up and waited in the lobby until 10:00 A.M. until someone finally remembered me."
> "They gave me a perfunctory tour, and then everyone left for lunch. I stayed behind and answered the phone."
> "The former sales manager arrived at the office, dumped the files out of his trunk into mine, and said, 'Good luck.'"

These may sound like horror stories, but for many people they are all too real.

Among major corporations, Hewlett-Packard does a wonderful job of bringing new employees on board. All new employees attend an extensive orientation session. Along with learning about benefits, they hear stories about the company's beginnings and are introduced to the company values firsthand by top managers. This initiation into the corporate community creates a strong sense of belonging.

Helping people belong requires that we create feelings of synergy and unity of purpose. We neglect to do this because we don't know how to do it, and we think "the real work" is more important. But more to the point is that we don't acknowledge *the significance of our relationships with each other.* The quality of our relationships is absolutely critical to the success of what we are doing!

Reducing Fear by Valuing People

To improve performance on projects, reduce fears, minimize cliques, and reduce the likelihood of lawsuits, there are several things managers need to do actively and routinely.

Expressing Appreciation

Employees frequently comment, "I always hear when things go wrong. But when things go right, it's just expected." Managers can change this by making a conscious effort to show appreciation. Small forms of recognition mean a lot. Acknowledge individuals in front of others, send a note of appreciation, give special assignments that recognize the person's abilities, and verbally say thank you. Let bosses, peers, and employees know that you notice, care, and value what they have done.

It is also helpful to set up peer-appreciation programs. The employees in one office decided to buy a small bear that everyone calls the appreciation bear. Every week or so, the bear appears in someone's office with a note of thanks for an action that was taken. Then the recipient passes the bear on to someone else. Such little expressions of kindness and acknowledgment go a long way. Appreciation needs to happen at every level. It is hard to give when we do not receive.

Getting to Know Employees as Individuals

In a utility company of more than 300 employees, Rick, the executive, makes it a point to know the name of every employee. Rick does not naturally remember names—he takes a roster home at night to memorize them. But he makes a point to do this because he feels it is important to employees and to the ultimate success of his business.

A consultant friend convinced me of the importance of our taking time to connect with one another before jumping into a work project. Routinely, she asks individuals in her groups to introduce themselves and share one unknown fact about themselves. Managers sometimes resist this activity because they have worked together for years, but the results are amazing. People share personal stories and experiences and develop a much deeper appreciation for one another. Then they move into the task and complete it in less time and with more laughter than ever before.

Many organizations sponsor events for employees to socialize, celebrate, and get to know each other better. But too often these events are underutilized for the value they can bring. Employees tend to sit with friends and colleagues whom they already know and fail to become acquainted with other groups. Deliberate orchestration of activities is necessary for people to become better acquainted! Social bonding cannot be left completely to happenstance and spontaneity or it will not occur at a meaningful level.

Encouraging Disagreement

The first two actions of expressing appreciation and getting to know each other are important because they build a foundation of trust, communication, and mutual appreciation. Without this base, confronting problems and expressing concerns is problematic for the best of us.

When a problem, disagreement, or conflict surfaces, we need to talk about our concerns rather than hold back. Use the following statements to invite differences of opinion and feedback:

To Give Feedback to Bosses

"I have an opinion about this decision, but I am hesitant to express it. Do you want to hear my views on the situation?"
"I need to be reassured that there will be no reprisals if I tell you what I really think about this issue."

To Encourage Diverse Opinions in a Group

"We have talked about the benefits of this idea. Now let's talk about the risks and drawbacks that we haven't discussed."
"Who has an opinion that is vastly different from the majority in this room? Let's hear your views and see what we can learn that might help us."
"I have an opinion that is very different from everyone else's. Do you want to hear it?"

To Solicit Employee Input

"I would like your input on how the new program is working. I especially want to know what can be improved and where there are problems. Please speak up even if you think I won't like what you have to say. Your ideas, insights, and feedback are important to me."

Asking Questions that Do Not Intimidate Others

The way we ask a question determines whether we get an honest answer or an evasive reply. Real interest and curiosity invite more responses than anger or blame. Questions that begin with the words *why* and *who* are more threatening than questions that start with the words *what* and *how*. *Why* and *who* questions can imply that someone is to blame for the problem. Observe the difference in the following list of questions:

Why *and* Who *Questions*

"Why did this happen?"
"Who was here yesterday?"
"Who is working with the suppliers?"

"Why does this happen every Monday?"
"Why are you late?"

What *and* How *Questions*

"How did this occur?"
"What took place yesterday?"
"How can we improve our work with the suppliers?"
"What causes this to happen every Monday?"
"What happened?"

Even under stressful conditions, it is important to wait for complete responses, to ask more than one question, and to acknowledge and thank individuals for the information they offer especially when it is not what we want to hear.

Fear can be a great enemy or a great teacher. If we fail to acknowledge the power of fear, it will disguise the issues and cause us to mistrust one another. But if we are willing to face these same fears and learn from them, they will help us grow strong in our ability to deal with reality, resolve our differences, and value each other.

ACTION EXERCISES

Exercise 1: Learning From Mistakes—Level One

The purpose of this exercise is to help you learn to dissect complex mistakes and to prepare you for analyzing mistakes in your organization. Do not move on to Exercise 2 until you have completed this initial exercise! This is a discussion activity that is ideally done with a group but can also be completed by an individual.

1. Make a list of well-known incidents that are considered to be mistakes (Vietnam War, Bay of Pigs, Watergate, *Challenger*, etc.). Discuss one incident that you have some knowledge of.

2. Answer the following questions as factually as you can:

   • What was the sequence of events that took place?
   • Who were the participants?
   • Who were the spectators or passive participants?
   • What key decisions were made that are considered mistakes?
   • What contributed to the mistakes?

3. Speculate and discuss the following questions:

   • What were the motives behind the decisions made and actions taken?
   • Which motives were positive (well-intended)? Which were negative (self-serving)?

4. Speculate and discuss the following questions:

   • What attitudes and behaviors might have contributed to the decisions?
   • What might participants and observers have done to change the course of events?

5. Identify what lessons can be learned from the incident:

   • How could the mistakes have been stopped or avoided?
   • What different attitudes and behaviors were needed?
   • What conclusions and insights about fear can you make?

Exercise 2: Learning From Mistakes—Level Two

The purpose of this exercise is to learn from past mistakes rather than blame each other for the problems. This is a powerful activity and needs to be undertaken in a blame-free environment. It is ideally done with a group but can also be done by an individual. This exercise will be most effective if it is led by a trained facilitator. Before you begin, appoint an individual to monitor the group process to ensure that blame and defensiveness are not occurring. If blame comes into play, the role of the monitor is to point out that this is happening and ask the group to change its behavior.

1. Make a list of well-known incidents in your organization that are considered to be mistakes or failures (acquisition, restructuring, programs or products that failed, etc.). Discuss one incident that most of you were directly involved with.

2. Answer the following questions as factually as you can:
   - What was the sequence of events that took place?
   - Who were the participants? What was each person's role?
   - Who were the spectators or passive participants?
   - What key decisions were made that are considered mistakes?
   - What factors led to the mistakes (financial, credibility, opportunity, expectations, promises, etc.)?

3. Individually answer the following questions and discuss in-depth:
   - What were the motives behind the decisions made and actions taken?
   - Which motives were positive (well-intended)? Which were negative (self-serving)?

Important: Answer questions 3 and 4 only for yourself—not for others in the group!

4. Speculate and discuss the following questions:
   - What attitudes, behaviors, assumptions, and beliefs did you have that contributed to the mistakes?
   - What prevented you from taking action, changing direction, or speaking up?

5. Discuss lessons that can be learned from the incident.

   • How could the mistakes have been stopped or avoided?
   • What different attitudes and behaviors were needed?
   • What conclusions and insights about the incident can you make?

6. Identify changes you can make to prevent this type of situation in the future.

   • Individually, what changes do you want to make?
   • As a group, what changes do you want to make?

Exercise 3: Unearthing Solutions to Workplace Problems

The purpose of this exercise is to help you dig deeply into issues and not prejudge the solutions before you hear others' views. The exercise is not easy to do but will yield useful insights and often innovative solutions. Be sure to follow the instructions carefully for best results.

1. Select a problem in your work that continues to be difficult for you. (Do not select a personnel problem for this exercise.)
2. Identify four people who have direct knowledge about the problem, and schedule to meet with each person individually.
3. Interview these individuals. Use questions that start with the words *how* and *what. During the interview only ask questions.* Refrain from stating your opinions. Take notes. Spend at least twenty minutes with each person you interview. Thank each person for his or her information.
4. Summarize what you learned. Decide if you need more information to determine a solution. If so, set up additional interviews. If not, identify your solution.
5. Reflect on what you learned doing this activity. What insights did you gain? How did it feel to ask questions only and not give your opinion? Share your insights with a colleague.

4

Hidden Agendas in Business Decisions

Men are but children of a larger growth.

—John Dryden, English poet and dramatist

Phil, Derrick, and Bernie decide to start a business together. They struggle at first, but after a few years they have a profitable, well-known company. During the normal course of affairs, Phil is contacted by a larger corporation that might be interested in acquiring the company. He's excited, and dollar signs—lots of them—float before his eyes.

Phil decides to share this exciting prospect with Derrick but not with Bernie. As the two partners talk, they can see the possibilities. They start to daydream about the profits from the sale of the business. Soon they have decided that it should all go to the two of them, rather than being split three ways with Bernie. They reinforce each other and rationalize why this is OK. They quickly come to believe it.

The three started the company as equals, but suddenly Bernie is low man on the totem pole and is going to be left out. The hidden agenda—greed—has taken over.

Phil and Derrick call Bernie in for a company meeting, but the possibility of a sellout is never even mentioned! Instead, Phil raises the issue of redistributing the stock and changing compensation plans. Derrick tells Bernie that he "is not cutting it" and that they want to redeem his shares. Sure, there have been tensions among them before—that's an inevitable part of being in business together—but this is an unexpected blow for Bernie.

Bernie is suspicious and tries to figure out why he is being dumped. Several weeks later, he discovers paperwork proposing the sale of the company along with a financial sheet projecting millions of dollars in profit over the next five years.

Cooperation and collaboration are now impossible. Bernie files a lawsuit against Phil and Derrick. Eventually a settlement is reached, and Bernie leaves the company. The other two partners pay $185,000 in legal fees to protect their option to sell the company.

Four years later, the company is no longer in business. Instead, Phil and Derrick are working as regular employees for the corporation that was going to buy them out as the larger corporation found it fiscally wiser to buy their talents than to purchase their business. Their company was destroyed by hidden agendas.

The Myth of Logic in Decision Making

We believe that we are logical, rational beings who base our decisions on facts and data. The reality is that too many of our decisions are affected by personal motives. Our denied emotions—such as fear, anger, and insecurity—show up as hidden agendas and mixed messages that impact the quality of our business decisions. Specifically, the quality of our decisions is affected when personal motives are used to:

- Gain power and control.
- Delay a change that is threatening.
- Advance a specific project.
- Avoid exposure of a mistake.
- Sabotage another's success.

Business decisions about strategy, priorities, direction, and allocation of resources are not effective when emotional needs are calling the shots. The consequences of decisions based on personal agendas are significant and costly and result in:

- Neglect of important priorities
- Loss of market opportunity
- Untimely delays
- Escalating costs from unexpected problems
- Project failures

Additional by-products of personal motives and hidden agendas are mistrust, interpersonal conflicts, and turf protection. The following problems are examples of these hidden agendas at work.

Skepticism That Undermines Venture

A manager is hired to launch a new business venture. His background and skills are unique and greatly expand the services offered by the company. The new venture is different from business as usual. The manager is working on the "product of the future" that will lead the company into growth opportunities. However, the new product requires faster response time, higher levels of service, a longer sales cycle, and in-depth knowledge of the customer.

The old guard is skeptical about what the new manager is trying to achieve. They don't understand the new venture and secretly harbor doubts about its success. So they keep the manager out of their accounts, fail to show up for his meetings, and place his requests for support at the bottom of their lists. They are afraid that he will take away money from their budgets, screw up their accounts, and possibly succeed, thereby forcing them to change the way they do business.

The new manager feels isolated, discouraged, and disconnected. He sees the lack of support for the venture and knows his talents are not appreciated. The support and encouragement he needs to launch the new product do not exist. Every day the situation erodes his self-confidence and makes him wonder if he should be there. He speaks to his wife and friends at home, but at work the real issues are not addressed.

Skepticism, mistrust, and fear prevented this man and his company from succeeding with the new venture.

False Assumptions That Undermine Effectiveness

When we don't talk openly about what is going on, false assumptions and misunderstandings undermine business effectiveness.

A black male manager recruits a black woman to fill an important position. The manager and the woman are long-standing friends and there is an obvious bond between them. The other employees became envious when they see their manager giving special attention to the new employee. Suspicions arise and rumors begin to fly. People start to ask, "Why did he really hire her?" and "Are they having an affair?" Every time they meet behind closed doors or go to lunch, word spreads like wildfire. Enormous time and energy are spent speculating about the relationship, but no one talks directly to the manager or the employee about his or her perceptions. The basic question regarding an affair and the deeper issues of jealousy and favoritism are not discussed.

When an outside consultant is brought in to deal with the group's "morale problem," people talk openly about the situation and the real issues come out. It turns out that the manager and the employee are not having an affair, but they frequently seek each other's company for solace and support. As minorities, they feel isolated and unwelcome in the dominant, white-male culture. The manager also comes to understand that his staff needs more support and attention from him.

The hours of conversations and suspicions caused by the false assumptions in this situation cannot be underestimated. Enormous energy was wasted because no one would confront the real issues.

Mistrust That Derails Plans

Without the trust that comes from honest communication, the best plans in the world can fail. Trust is built on the belief that *I can count on you to do what you say; I can depend on you.* When we don't have trust, we build elaborate mechanisms to ensure, verify, and monitor the behavior of other people. We don't trust them to give us what we need.

An improvement team works for three months to find the fastest, most error-free way to process customer orders. They analyze the work process, brainstorm options, and identify solutions that will eliminate duplication and cut processing time in half. But as they talk about their ideas, there is a sense of futility and despair. No one is excited about the likely outcome. What is wrong? Why such discouragement?

The solutions reached by the improvement team involve reassigning responsibility for paperwork from field sales people to home office personnel. The changes make logical sense and will eliminate much duplication of effort. But there is so much distrust between the field salespeople and home office people that the solution is bound to fail. Home office employees do not trust the field salespeople to give them accurate information, and the field salespeople do not trust the home office employees to handle their customers right and not "screw up the account."

Lack of trust is the real issue. All the plans for improvement in this process will fail if trust is not established between the two groups. The team's initial solution does not deal with the real issue. Trust must be established before the solution will work.

Greed That Creates Turf

Greed is one of the toughest issues to deal with. Greed is the desire to take more than our share. No matter how much we have, it is never enough. We continually try to get more. *Greed is a desperate need to have something outside ourselves to make us feel important.* It is the ultimate con man of our vulnerabilities. In business, we silently condone the needy, grabbing behaviors of greed. We even encourage them. To stop greed, we must first acknowledge the emptiness inside before it is possible to change the feelings and correct the behaviors.

In business, greed can take the form of hoarding projects, not sharing information, or protecting political contacts so we feel important. Amazingly, many people are able to pull it off, resulting in turf wars as we protect our budgets, projects, interests, and political contacts from others.

Greed is subtle and takes us before we know it. When greed rears its head, we immediately rationalize why what we are doing is OK. The senior management team in a marketing and promotion business promises employees a percentage bonus based on the achievement of ambitious profit goals. Much to the managers' amazement, employees far exceed the goals. When the managers calculate the bonus payment that is due employees, greed sets in and they renege on their agreement, choosing instead to pay only the amount they initially anticipated, not the actual percentage bonus earned. One manager refuses to cooperate with what he calls the unethical behavior of his peers. As a result, he is terminated.

We can tell when greed is present by the telltale sign of our willingness to do almost anything to get more of whatever we're after. The ends justify the means. Shabby motives dress up in lofty language. Agreements are made in secret, and we begin to hide our cards, play close to the vest, and try to beat our opponents. We recognize greed in others, but almost never in ourselves.

Actions to Take When Facing Hidden Agendas

When faced with hidden agendas of greed, turf protection, mistrust, or sabotage, the following are types of statements that can be made to describe what you think is going on and to ask for a change:

> "I am not comfortable with the decision that is being proposed. I'm worried that there may be hidden agendas involved. Can we talk about this?"
>
> "There is a lot of private speculation and conversation going on behind closed doors about this issue. I wonder if we might talk more openly about our real concerns."
>
> "I receive a lot of support verbally for this project, but no one shows up for my meetings, wants to spend time on the project, or indicates much interest. Can we talk about what you are really thinking?"
>
> "You seem worried. Is the pending reorganization (decision, change, etc.) bothering you?"
>
> "We used to get along well but once I was promoted to supervisor, all that changed. I was wondering if we might go have coffee and talk about how we both feel and get things back on track."

The following is a list of actions you can take to address hidden agendas and covert issues:

- Refuse to talk about a problem unless the people directly involved are included in the discussion as well.
- Set up a meeting and invite all parties to come and share their views openly.
- Refuse to carry rumors or speculate.
- Ask direct questions about suspected motives and hidden agendas, for example, "Do you want my job?" or "Do you disagree with the decision?"
- Publish rumors in weekly news bulletins and counter them with facts.
- Invite employees to talk about rumors. Then have an open discussion about the issues and concerns that are on people's minds.
- Invite people to acknowledge hidden concerns when important decisions are being made.
- Set aside a special time on a regular basis for people to share their questions and concerns. This simple checking-in procedure will stop rumors before they start.

Emotional Needs vs. Business Decisions

To deal with hidden agendas, we must learn to separate emotional needs from business decisions. Emotional needs are the domain of the child within us. That makes these needs important, not unimportant. But when our emotional needs are in charge of the business, it's the equivalent of letting a child drive the family car.

The adult must have the wisdom to recognize and address emotional needs and simultaneously make good business decisions. Business decisions, such as deciding what products to offer, must be based on customer needs—not on whether we like the person proposing the new product. Job openings should be filled by the person best qualified for the job—not because we feel guilty or owe somebody something. Business decisions must be distinguished from emotional needs, but not completely separated from them. *The challenge is to simultaneously make good business decisions and tend to emotional needs.*

We don't have the right balance between these two dimensions today. The scale is either tipped too heavily toward making bottom-line decisions or, conversely, tipped too heavily toward meeting emotional needs. Just as an organization cannot thrive if it negates emotions, neither can it prosper if it solely responds to emotional needs. There are very few models of organizations that manage both dimensions well.

Decision Entanglements

Sometimes hidden agendas become standard practice rather than an occasional occurrence. When this happens, we go round and round about decisions but never seem to get anywhere. Endless discussions are a primary symptom of emotional needs getting confused with business decisions.

One manager describes it like this: "We meet and talk endlessly about options and possibilities, but we don't seem to be able to reach any conclusions. The decisions we make never go anywhere. We can't implement once we decide. It's like we're impotent. We can't make anything happen."

Confusion occurs when business decisions and emotional needs become indistinguishable. The issues run together and all decisions become complicated, hard to make, and basically unworkable. This type of dynamics is often found in family-owned businesses, businesses among friends, romantic relationships at work, and any type of codependent bonding. It's not that these combinations can't work—it's that we are more vulnerable to confusion when involved in them.

Symptoms of the Problem

How do you know when you are not adequately separating organizational decisions from emotional needs? There are some obvious clues. You tend to:

- Tread lightly around certain issues or avoid them altogether.
- Not feel free to suggest specific solutions.

- Try many different solutions but none of them work.
- Complain bitterly but are unable to take action.
- See new options as too complicated to implement.
- Always hope things will change and get better.
- Feel you are between a rock and a hard place.

The feelings of the people involved are of two types. Some individuals feel smothered, controlled, dependent, anxious, and unappreciated. Others feel frustrated, angry, irritated, hand-tied, and overworked. All parties do not feel empowered to change the situation. It's like being caught in the middle of a rubber band: All action takes you back to the middle and nothing changes! People in this dynamic try many external solutions, but *nothing can change until the underlying dynamic changes.*

Feeling Trapped—and Getting Out

If you are in this type of situation, you can't deal with it alone. It is too volatile and entrenched. *The solution requires new behaviors and decisions that the existing patterns do not allow.* What is needed is a trusted outside person to guide you out of the situation. Trust is important because everything in the dynamic will pull you back into it!

The following are guidelines for selecting a consultant to help you. The consultant:

- Is a neutral third party.
- Is not perceived to be on anyone's side!
- Has credentials and background in psychology.
- Has experience in business decision making.
- Has no bias about the decisions the group should make.
- Expects the group to address the issues openly versus works strictly one-on-one.
- Has the reputation for keeping confidences.
- Does not create indefinite dependency on his or her services.

Releasing ourselves from entanglement requires changing the game. As we start to do this, it feels very unsafe. We must act in ways that upset old patterns and shed new light on the situation that exists. But the real danger is remaining in the dynamic. Group meetings and decision points become sinkholes that drain vital energy and attention away from work that is needed. Eventually, implosion occurs and the whole thing caves in—someone leaves, relationships break, the company folds, etc. Then everyone loses.

It is possible to change the dynamic without destroying the company or doing irrevocable harm to relationships. And it is gratifying when the dynamic gradually changes and individuals are able to perform again. The business issues and personal needs must slowly be unraveled and each one addressed with integrity and care.

Separating Facts From Feelings

The following are steps you can take as part of a management team to separate business needs and personal needs:

1. Acknowledge the presence of strong feelings.
2. Clarify individual feelings and needs.
3. Identify and respect the needs of the business.
4. Create a win-win solution for individuals, and the organization.
5. Be truthful and compassionate in the process.

Acknowledging the Presence of Strong Feelings

The key to unraveling the situation is to separate the emotional needs from the business needs, but you must begin the process by acknowledging that you have a problem. Agree to meet on a regular basis to discuss the relevant issues and make decisions about the best course of action to take. It is important to give yourself uninterrupted time.

Clarifying Individual Feelings and Needs

To unravel the present, you must revisit the past and address the unmet expectations, hurts, and outdated agreements before you can move forward. Details of this step, which involve recreating the organizational history as well as the history of each individual on the team, are presented in Action Exercise 2 at the end of this chapter. This step is an essential building block that enables group members to understand how group dynamics and company priorities evolved. Once the past is understood, group members can discuss how it is influencing the present. At this point the difficult issues are discussed. Individuals talk about expectations that have not been met, disappointments along the way, and mistrust that has developed over time. Each person shares his or her own perspective uninterrupted by others except for questions. Once personal needs, disappointments, and expectations are openly shared, individuals are more willing to accommodate what needs to be done from a business point of view.

Identifying and Respecting the Needs of the Business

Now the group must focus on the needs of the business, agreeing upon its key issues and priorities. The group members list the areas they agree on and select areas to address and solve. Many of the former disputes will be seen from a new perspective and with greater understanding because of the sharing that took place in the earlier steps.

Creating a Win-Win Solution

Decisions are made about ways to address business needs and personal needs. Roles may be altered, projects may be dropped, new structures may be put in place, or the way decisions are made may be changed. The final step is to develop action plans that reflect the decisions just made and determine who will do what by when. Throughout the discussion, it is important to believe that win-win solutions can be created for individuals, for the team, and for the business.

Being Truthful and Compassionate in the Process

The most challenging part of this process is to trust each other and tell the truth. The review of the history is critical in this regard because it places individual needs in a larger context and increases trust and understanding among team members. To address the issues we need to lay aside our egos, false assumptions, and resentments and address the real needs. We must be willing to listen to others as well as speak up for ourselves.

ACTION EXERCISES

Exercise 1: Addressing Hidden Agendas

The purpose of this exercise is to help you deal with a hidden agenda at work.

1. Identify a situation where you feel that you or a decision you are involved with is being impacted by hidden agendas. Write down what you can say to talk openly about the issue.
2. Practice your comments with a friend and receive feedback.
3. When you are ready, confront the situation.

Exercise 2: Unraveling Entangled Decision Making

The purpose of this exercise is to help a management team unravel the impact of their history and past relationships on important decisions that they need to make today.

1. Review your history together.

   - Draw an organizational time line.
   - Discuss your history and the changes that have taken place.
   - Identify challenges the companies has faced.
   - Identify what was required in the past for success versus now.

2. Discuss how you came together as a team.

   - How did each person become a member and when on the time line?
   - What did each individual want to give the team?
   - What did each individual expect to receive from the team?

3. Discuss how the past is influencing the present.

   - What expectations have been met or not met? What disappointments exist?
   - How are yesterday's expectations impacting today's relationships?

4. Identify and separate current business needs and personal needs.

   - What are the current needs and expectations of team members?
   - What are the current business needs and priorities?
   - Where is or isn't there a fit between business needs and individual needs? Between individual needs and team needs?

5. Engage in action planning.

   - What solutions are needed to meet individual, team, and business needs?
   - What are constructive options to address a mismatch between individual needs and organizational needs?
   - What actions need to be taken to implement the solutions?

5

Hot Buttons That Trigger Conflicts

Hating people is like burning down your own house to get rid
of a rat.

—Harry Emerson Fosdick, U.S. clergyman

Skyler: Jake, have you finished that marketing report yet? I need
to use it for a management presentation that's coming up.
I hope it's done.

Jake: Are you crazy? You know I'm working full-time on the
trade show. I'm up to my eyeballs in deadlines. There's no
way I can get to that report right now—or anytime in the
near future.

Skyler: What! I was counting on you. I've got to have that report
for my presentation! This is a very important meeting.
The VPs are coming in from out of town and it's critical
that they see the new strategy.

Jake: Here! *[He tosses a file onto Skyler's desk.]* The data is in here.
Dig it out for yourself. You can get your hands dirty like
the rest of us!

What Are Hot Buttons?

Volatile interactions occur at work when we activate each other's
hot buttons. *Hot buttons are intense emotional reactions to specific peo-*

ple, events, or situations that are caused by personal vulnerabilities. Someone says or does something, our gut tightens, and we turn inside out. We respond by closing up, striking out, withdrawing, or yelling. A hot button can be activated in a second. In the earlier example, Jake's hot button is his belief that he does all the dirty work, and Skyler gets all the glory.

Hot buttons are our instinctive reactions to situations that create strong feelings inside us. *They are the consequence of past hurts more than present reality.* Hot buttons do not take place on a rational level but rather at the primal, survival level. We react instantly and unconsciously to a behavior or person, unaware of what is causing the intensity of our feelings and behaviors. We believe that someone or something out there is making us angry and upset rather than the emotions inside ourselves.

Hot buttons are set off by different experiences. One person's reaction is triggered by a lie, another's is triggered by the loss of an opportunity, and still another's is triggered by the dynamics that occur in a meeting. When these strong emotions are activated, our response goes far beyond what the situation requires. We become rigid and lose our ability to act effectively. The more intense the vulnerability, the hotter our reactions. Each of us goes to work with our own unique hot buttons. They cannot be removed; they are part of what makes us who we are.

Hot Buttons in Action

[1]

Matt, the supervisor of a production department, calls Jack, one of his foremen, into his office.

Matt: Jack, I want you to stop yelling at the employees on the line.

Jack: What are you talking about?

Matt: I had three complaints last week. You're coming on too strong and intimidating them. You've got to ease up.

Jack: I get the job done. No one is able to get these people to produce the kind of results I do.

Matt: Jack—this is serious. You have to ease up. It could cost you your job if you don't.

Matt is utterly amazed at what happens next.

Jack: My job! If *that's* what you're talking about—*I quit!* I don't need this crap.

Matt is stunned. Jack's resignation is completely unexpected. As for Jack, he is terrified that Matt will judge him as undesirable and unworthy. Jack cannot tolerate being seen as a poor performer. When Matt's reprimand brings up these uncomfortable feelings, Jack's hot button is triggered and he resigns. Jack goes from job to job rather than deal with the feelings of shame he experiences when confronted with his unacceptable actions.

[2]

Steve is a successful internal consultant, working at the highest levels in the organization. However, he does not have a reputation for teamwork with his peers. Over lunch one day, he talks with Janelle, another internal consultant.

Janelle: How's it going, Steve?

Steve: I'm exhausted. I worked all weekend summarizing the data I collected after four days of interviewing the executives. There's still so much to do. I have to eat and run so I can get ready for the president's staff meeting tomorrow.

Janelle: Can I help you in any way? I'm not as under the gun as you and it would be good for me to get some exposure to the leaders around here. Perhaps we could work on the project together.

Steve: No way! The executives wouldn't tolerate a new person coming in at this late date. I'm the only one they trust. I can't let them down. Besides, I'm almost done with the report. Thanks anyway.

Steve's hot button is that he feels inadequate unless he is seen as the best, the brightest, and most recognized person in the work unit. He sacrifices weekends and himself in order to maintain his position of importance, then he resents the lack of support from others. Steve's competitive needs keep him from working collaboratively or receiving help from others.

[3]

We may know people for years and never see their hot buttons. Then one day we say or do something and fireworks are set off.

Mary is a hard worker in a small law firm. She is known as the gentlest of people, never getting angry and always helping everyone with his or her problems. For fifteen years she has successfully planned, anticipated, and handled the administrative needs of the five lawyers in the firm. Last week, Rob, one of the newest lawyers, decided to hire a temporary person to help him complete a special assignment. He has no idea that Mary is terribly hurt because she was not consulted about the decision.

Rob: Mary, can you come into my office for a moment?
Mary: Sure. I'll be there in a second.

[Fifteen minutes later]

Rob: Oh, Mary, I'm glad to see you. There's a customer call that might be coming in this afternoon. I want to brief you on the situation so you can handle it if I'm not available.
Mary: That would be fine but I won't be here this afternoon. Remember, you asked me to go down to the courthouse to retrieve information on the Jackson case. I was planning to leave after lunch.

Rob: Oh, that's right. I forgot. Well, call the temp in here. I'll ask her to do it.

Mary [*with a tight lip*]: Fine! I'll go get her.

Mary stomps out of Rob's office, takes off her shoes, and throws them, one after another, through the door at his head. An unexpected hot button has been triggered.

[4]

Chris, the information manager in a large medical facility, is continually frustrated with the performance of Bill, one of his programmers. He stops in to talk about his concerns with Beverly, the human resources director.

Beverly: Hi, Chris, it's nice to see you. What's on your mind?

Chris: I'm concerned about Bill. You know, the dark-haired guy who's kind of quiet.

Beverly: Sure, I know Bill. What's the problem?

Chris: Let's see. How can I describe this to you?

Beverly: Is he doing something that's bothering you?

Chris: Well, yes. He's always late. He does half the volume of work as my other programmers. And he doesn't really fit in with the group.

Beverly: Have you talked to him about this?

Chris: No, actually I haven't. I was hoping you would talk to him. I don't know where to begin. Besides, I think he would take it better coming from you. I know him too well.

Chris's hot button is fear of confrontation and the need to be liked at all costs. Chris grew up in a family where he was not allowed to express anger or disapproval of any kind. Now, he avoids any situation where he needs to confront others directly. He wants to be the one everyone likes, so he asks Beverly to take care of the problem so he won't have to do it.

The Effect of Hot Buttons

Every day we are surrounded by people we must work with closely. In confined spaces, under tense working conditions, it is easy to irritate one another. There are people whose very existence sets us off. We react strongly to their presence, and conflict, suspicion, and mistrust are just below the surface. We learn to walk around and sidestep these land mines, avoiding certain topics or approaches. Then, suddenly, an action takes place, the dynamite goes off—and we may have no idea how things got started! Our hot buttons become trip-wires that set off emotional explosions when we do not recognize or accept our vulnerabilities.

Yet dealing with hot buttons can take a lot of time and energy and distract us from doing the work needed. Hot buttons impact business in the following ways:

- Individuals refuse to work with each other.
- Important communication does not occur.
- Decisions are made for the wrong reason.
- Power struggles take place.
- Projects are delayed or thwarted.

Emotional hot buttons also limit our options. When our vulnerabilities are present, it is hard for us to consider and experiment with new behaviors. Instinctively, we feel danger, and our emotional reactions tell us that there is a threat against which we must protect ourselves. From a reactive position, we insist on doing things one way—the way we have always done them before—the way we know. It takes great courage to change our behaviors when we feel emotionally vulnerable.

Once I conducted an assessment for a client who had the reputation of not listening to women consultants. My male colleagues suggested that they present the assessment results to the client, but I wouldn't hear of it. Having my colleagues present the data was a personal insult to me. As a child I grew up feeling dominated and negated by a highly opinionated father, so one of my hot buttons is "not being heard." I could not even consider their suggestion. All I could do was react and say no. Hot buttons limit our ability to be flexible and consider multiple options for the best solution.

When someone or something touches off our hot buttons, we don't want to be near them. We don't like having our vulnerabilities accessed—more accurately, we don't like the feelings inside ourselves—and we don't like being out of control, so we distance ourselves from the people, activities, and circumstances that activate our hot buttons. We turn down risky assignments and shy away from volatile topics. Entire organizations and job assignments are restructured to avoid specific problems and people. The real issues are not addressed.

It is true that hot buttons can provide strong motivation, but they operate in this way for only a limited period of time. Eventually, their power wears out. Our needs demand to be satisfied by genuine caring rather than compensated for by money, success, or power. As the motivational effect of hot buttons starts to diminish, we discover that our achievements no longer satisfy us, work becomes meaningless, former dreams and goals seem pointless, and power is no longer a thrill. What used to drive us to succeed no longer holds any meaning.

Our hot buttons go with us into every job, relationship, and work experience. Even after we have learned to recognize these reactions, they are still present and we remain vulnerable to them. We can hide and deny them, but when tensions are high and fear emerges, our hot buttons are always the first ones to show up for the performance!

Recognizing Hot Buttons

When a person's behavior activates a hot button, our bodies sound an alarm. We experience a fear-based reaction. Our jaws tighten, voices elevate, eyes widen, and movements become rigid and restrained. Everything in us seems to contract. We attempt to remove ourselves from the vulnerable feelings by withdrawing, blaming others, or denying the situation that needs to be addressed. We hide from the vulnerabilities that cause our reactions. The feelings associated with our hot buttons are too raw, too hurtful, and too shameful for us to face.

We can recognize personal hot buttons by their intensity and consistent presence in our lives. The following are indicators that we are dealing with a hot button, either our own or someone else's. We continually:

- Complain and feel frustrated about circumstances.
- Wish we could be free of a person or situation.
- Obsess about trying to figure out another person's motives.
- Plan endless strategies for dealing with a person or situation.
- Structure time so we don't have to deal with a person or issue.
- Talk a lot to others about a person behind their back.
- Feel helpless and believe that nothing will work.

Hot buttons create predictable, almost scripted reactions. Like a broken record, we hear ourselves saying, "They don't appreciate me," "I always take the blame," or "They never listen." Those who know us can anticipate how we will react. No matter where we are, what we are doing, or whom we are working with, when our hot buttons get pushed, we sing the same old tired song over and over again—until we find a new tune.

Keeping Hot Buttons From Taking Control

We need to find a way to deal with our hot buttons. If we do not, we will continually be frustrated by the conflicts we experience.

To repair the unhealthy dynamics caused by hot buttons, we must change ourselves first. There may be short-term remedies like a vacation from work that appease the situation, but there are no lasting solutions until we work from the inside out. We must stop seeking solutions from other people and start accepting our role in the drama before tensions will dissolve. Looking inside is hard work: It's easier to blame others and want them to change. But this strategy never brings results. When we want lasting solutions to interpersonal conflicts, there are critical steps we need to take:

1. *Stop* our reactions and trying to change the other person.
2. *Sort out* the situation and identify our personal needs.
3. *Shift* our attitudes toward others to solve the problem.

Step One: Stop

The first step in dealing with our hot buttons is to *stop* the chain of reaction that occurs. We think about the person or situation incessantly. We talk about the problem with anyone who is sympathetic to our cause. We develop strategies, engage in overt conflict, justify our behaviors, seek support, anticipate the person's next move, protect ourselves, make resolutions, and think about the situation at night instead of connecting with our family, relaxing, or eating supper. The goal of this obsessive behavior is to gain the upper hand and get what we want.

We must literally STOP using our personal time and energy to think about the other person and plan what we are going to do next. We must STOP trying to get them to be or do what we want. This is very difficult to achieve. We don't want to stop. We don't think we should stop. Our first response is: "Yes, but this situation requires me to do something. There is no way I can just stand by and let this happen." We are afraid the other person might win or not change if we don't take action. After all, if we don't stand up for what's right, who will? We don't want to give up fighting for what we need. That would make us feel too helpless.

Withdrawal is an enormous first step. A big part of us wants—even needs—to keep the drama going. On an unconscious level, we are attracted to the conflict. That's the nature of hot buttons: They are deeply embedded in our psyches, and we resist giving them up. The idea of focusing on ourselves seems antithetical to what we are trying to achieve. After all, in our clouded state of mind, *we* aren't causing the problem—*they* are. But the truth is that the only person in the world we can change is ourselves. When we change how we feel, react, and think, we increase the likelihood that others will change also. *When we change, others change.*

Let's see how hot buttons affected the management team at one corporation.

Dick and Katheryn are the president and vice president of an agricultural division in a large corporation. The R&D group has recently discovered a product that will eliminate the need for a costly additive that is currently being used to boost production. Most of the development work is done, patents are in place, and it is time to create the structures that will distribute and sell the new product.

Initially, things go well. Katheryn and Dick have a history of working together and respect each other's abilities. But as pressure mounts to get the new product out the door, hot buttons take control.

Dick is on the road every week and is difficult to contact. Many decisions are delayed until he returns to give his input and blessing. Dick likes to shoot from the hip and forms his opinions based on intuitive data gathered from his experience in the field.

Katheryn resents Dick for his dogmatic opinions and doesn't think he listens to her point of view. She believes that he uses input from the field to discount the marketing data she presents to him. When Katheryn disagrees with Dick, he gets angry and impatient with her and storms around the office. Dick resents Katheryn's need for detail and feels thwarted by her lack of enthusiasm for his ideas.

Katheryn responds to stress by taking control. She reviews and edits all letters that go out and insists that reports receive her final approval before being distributed. Many times she feels that the success of the company rests solely on her shoulders.

As their emotional needs become volatile, the once effective partners lose their ability to manage well. Dick makes decisions to show Katheryn that she can't micromanage the business; Katheryn ignores Dick's good ideas because "he doesn't listen to anyone else." Staff meetings are unproductive as communication and decisions become laced with tense emotions.

Both Dick and Katheryn lose sight of the value they once saw in each other and begin to focus instead on what they aren't getting. Each wants the other to change so he or she can feel better. They finally stop talking to each other and find ways to be out of the office in a desperate attempt to cool down the situation.

The first step for Katheryn and Dick to address their hot buttons is to stop their reactions and stop trying to change each other.

Step Two: Sort Out

The second step in dealing with hot buttons is *sorting out* all the feelings we are having.

Sorting out helps us stop seeing the problem as something "they" are doing to us and start seeing the problem as one we own. We can sort out the situation by asking ourselves these questions:

- What do I like and dislike about this situation?
- What expectations and assumptions are causing me to react so strongly?
- What vulnerabilities are being touched?
- How am I contributing to the dynamics?
- What fears do I have?
- What needs do I have that are not being met?
- How is this situation similar to conflicts I have experienced in the past?

The purpose of sorting out is to move past our reactions to find the root cause of what is bothering us. Unless we identify our vulnerabilities and meet these needs, we will not be able to change our behavior.

Here's how Katheryn and Dick examined their personal histories to sort out their feelings.

When Katheryn and Dick take time to sort out their individual needs, childhood experiences provide important clues to the dynamics. Dick grew up in a family where he was considered different and his "wild ideas" were not appreciated. Consequently, he feels an intense need to have his intuitive opinions heard and validated. Privately, Dick realizes he questions the value of his ideas. He makes a commitment to affirm his own opinions and listen to the views of others.

Katheryn grew up in a family where she was expected to take over as the mom. She learned early to be the one in charge. Katheryn realizes she needs to let go of the demanding expectations she has of herself and others. She relaxes her grip and starts to share more responsibility as well as credit with employees, and upon occasion, she even makes fun of herself.

Change does not come overnight, but Katheryn and Dick are now alert to their vulnerabilities and recognize when hot buttons are interfering in their relationship. Hidden needs are no longer in control of their business effectiveness.

Here's another case—this one about Tom, a frustrated supervisor, who is an example of the positive changes that can happen when we sort out our own needs before problem solving with others.

Tom is miserable as a supervisor. He resents the time he has to spend on morale issues and trying to keep people happy. He feels burned out and angry about all the personnel issues that come up and wishes his employees would "just grow up." Tom's management style doesn't work for his employees either. They describe him as "distant," "controlling," "an ineffective delegate," and "a poor communicator." Tom is ready to give up supervision and go back to being an individual contributor.

Tom's first step is to stop reacting to his employees' behavior and start focusing on his own needs. So far, his attempts to change them have not been successful. Although he can't see a solution, Tom accepts the idea that he will benefit by examining his own behavior.

Before becoming a supervisor, Tom loved conducting research, drawing diagrams, analyzing data, and discussing technical issues with colleagues. Now, as a supervisor, the only things he enjoys are the professional meetings he attends with peers. In these meetings Tom is a natural leader. But back at the office, he returns to the "grind" of managing people.

Tom reflects on these questions:

- What do I like and dislike about being a supervisor?
- What expectations and assumptions do I have about my role?
- How am I contributing to the problem?
- What needs do I have that are not being met?
- How is this experience similar to others that I have encountered?
- What hurts or memories in my life are being activated by this situation?

Answering these questions leads to important insights for Tom.

As a supervisor, Tom believes that he must deny his own needs. He assumes it is his role to "make employees happy." Tom grew up in a family where his parents set aside their needs to take care of the children. His parents' activities, schedules, and priorities were dictated by the needs of the kids. Tom realizes he is basing his supervisory style on the role model he received from his parents. Unconsciously, he negates and ignores his own needs. Given these expectations, it is no wonder that Tom resents employee demands and wants to quit.

Tom makes a list of his needs and the actions he can take by answering these questions:

- What do I need and want from this situation?
- What can I control and what can't I control?
- What changes can I personally make?

Tom realizes he wants to use his technical ability as well as manage people. To meet this need, he initiates a discussion group on professional issues in the department and becomes involved in new projects that are technically challenging to him. Over time he accepts the fact that not all his decisions make others happy. He stops playing the role of dutiful parent and finds ways to enjoy what he is doing.

To solve the problems we have with other people, we must identify and meet our own emotional needs before we ask others to meet them. Our demands that others meet our needs frequently boomerang back to us. We want someone to appreciate us—and they blame us for a problem. We want to be noticed for a project that goes well— and others don't even know we worked on it. We try to help someone out—and they are ungrateful. Rarely do we get what we want from other people *unless we are first giving it to ourselves*. When our needs boomerang, they boomerang back to us so we can meet them.

Step Three: Shift

In this step we change our attitudes toward others to improve the situation. *Shifting* means the goal is no longer to win or to prove other people wrong. We stop thinking about "our" side and "their" side. Events and misconceptions that occurred in the past are discussed and then let go so we can move forward. Yes, their actions have hurt us, but we know that if we continue to focus on the hurt, winning is impossible. Shifting means:

- Moving away from blame to a place of empathy
- Trusting that a mutual solution is possible
- Accepting what we need
- Asking for what we want
- Being willing to work side by side to solve the problem

In the act of shifting we reconnect with the other person or people and work to find solutions that are mutually beneficial—for us, for them, and for the organization. We are willing to understand their needs and points of view just as we have understood our own. They are no longer "the villain." They are people—like us—who have needs that are not being met. We reconnect with the following attitudes:

- I want to listen to your point of view.
- I understand and appreciate your needs, even when they conflict with mine.
- I am willing to work with you until we can find a solution.

Here's what Tom did in the process of shifting.

After Tom completes his internal process, he is ready to reconnect with his staff. Tom invites his employees to share their views with him. At first, they are suspicious. But as he listens, they start to open up and talk about their frustration with work assignments. In the past, Tom would have reacted and felt they did not appreciate his efforts. Now he states his own needs and asks for suggestions on ways to work things out. Employees can feel the shift that has taken place in Tom's attitude. He is now receptive to their points of view. They are able to work together and reach agreements. Over time, through patience and practice, Tom becomes an excellent manager and coach who is respected and appreciated by his employees.

Additional Actions to Take

The following are additional actions you can take to reduce the effect of hot buttons:

- Learn to laugh at your reactions and make fun of your reactive behaviors. Exaggerate them—really overdo it—with a friend who laughs with you.
- Find easy ways to connect with your "adversary." Stop by his or her desk and ask for a paper clip. Any neutral behavior that makes a connection will do. Do this once a day until it becomes comfortable.
- Begin to say nice things about the person to others. You will be amazed how well this works to change your attitude and his or hers.
- Practice "emotional Tai Chi." When the person says or does something that throws you off balance, learn to flow with your reactions rather than tensing up. This response takes practice but is very gratifying when you can do it.
- Stop talking to other people about the problem or the person. Avoid people who keep the fight going or enjoy your complaints. Spend time with people who encourage you to talk about yourself, not the other person.
- Draw a picture that illustrates the current situation and your reactions (stick figures work great). Then draw a picture of how you want the relationship to work. This is a fun and very powerful change technique.

Summary

Business relationships are much like marriages. In the beginning, the romance of what is possible is strong enough to hold things together. But as the reality of working together occurs, hot buttons emerge. Most of our conflicts with people at work are born out of our need to get them to do something different. However, when we are dependent on another person to change, the situation tends to deteriorate. Making someone else change is like asking him or her to give us a present when he or she doesn't want to.

The benefits of addressing our hot buttons are improved relationships, more correct decisions, and better managed projects. We no longer waste time avoiding certain people, engaging in conflicts, or defending our position—but rather we enjoy the diversity of opinions, ideas, and solutions that take place because we are working with people we trust.

ACTION EXERCISES

Exercise 1: Identifying Hot Buttons

The purpose of this exercise is to help you recognize when hot buttons are present.

1. Reflect on your work situation and check whether you are continually experiencing the following behaviors:

   _____ I frequently complain and feel frustrated about a person or situation.

   _____ I wish I were completely free of or removed from a person or situation.

   _____ I obsessively try to figure out another person's motives.

   _____ I plan endless strategies for dealing with a person or situation.

   _____ I structure time so I don't have to deal with a person or situation.

   _____ I frequently talk to others about a person behind his or her back.

   _____ I feel helpless and believe that nothing will work.

   _____ I think the role of this person is to thwart me.

   _____ I hear myself making the same complaint over and over.

   _____ There is only one way I can respond to this person or situation.

   _____ I am shocked by the intensity of my reaction to a person or situation.

   _____ I work especially hard to win this person's approval.

   _____ The situation is taking time and attention away from productive work.

2. Identify current or past situations when your hot buttons were activated.
3. Write down situations where you saw others' hot buttons in action.

Exercise 2: Defusing Hot Buttons

The purpose of this exercise is to help you defuse hot buttons and engage in a way that is collaborative. The steps below refer to people but also apply to situations.

1. Stop reacting to or trying to change the other person.

   - What reactions and behaviors can you stop doing?
   - How can you stop reacting to a person you don't like?

2. Sort out your reactions to the person and identify what you can do. First answer these questions:

   - What do I like and dislike about this person?
   - What expectations and assumptions are causing me to react so strongly?
   - What vulnerabilities are being touched? What fears do I have?
   - How is the situation with this person similar to what I have experienced in the past?
   - How am I contributing to the dynamics?

Finish the sorting process by answering three important questions:

   - What do I want and need?
   - What can I control and what can't I control?
   - What changes can I personally make?

3. Shift to reconnect and work collaboratively with the other person. Identify three specific ways to show respect for differences, listen to the other person's perspective, and communicate your willingness to cooperate.

Exercise 3: Accepting Responsibility for Your Own Life*

The purpose of this exercise is to increase responsibility for your own life. This assignment is tough but will provide you with important insights if you complete it as directed.

1. Identify an incident at work that you did not like. Write down the event in the space above the box.

The incident:

How I contributed to the problem	How others contributed to the problem

*I am indebted to John Enright, a business consultant, for this activity.

2. Draw an arrow vertically through the box to indicate the degree to which you feel responsible for the problem. The space to the left is your degree of responsibility; the space to the right indicates the degree to which you believe others contributed to the problem.

3. Under the left side of the box, write down specifically how you contributed to the problem (I thought, forgot, neglected, assumed, etc.). Under the right side of the box, write down specifically how others contributed to the problem (they said, did, forgot, denied, made, etc.). At this point you have a description of who did what to create the problem.

The incident:

How I contributed to the problem	How others contributed to the problem

- I forgot . . .
- I thought . . .
- I neglected . . .

- They said . . .
- They did . . .
- They forgot . . .

4. Now repeat the exercise and assume responsibility for the entire box. This is challenging, but try to do it. Write down all the things you could have done to prevent the problems on the right that were created by someone or something else.

The incident:

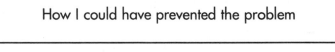

How I could have prevented the problem

- I could have said . . .
- I could have looked . . .
- I could have stopped . . .

- They said . . .
- They did . . .
- They forgot . . .

5. Finally, without blaming yourself, identify why you did not take these actions (did not have the skill, permission, time, willingness, etc.).
6. Summarize and discuss what you learned from doing this activity.

   - What insights do you have?
   - What changes can you make?
   - What attitudes/behaviors are in your way?

6

Corporate Craziness

"It's not only the scenery you miss by going too fast—you also miss the sense of where you are going and why."

—Eddie Cantor, entertainer

There is a lot of craziness inside organizations today. People work incredibly long hours, frantically completing paperwork and projects that produce no results. An executive manager in a utility company reflects on her experience after leaving a high-level job: "I can hardly believe how caught up I got in the craziness. I worked seventy to eighty-five–hour workweeks, and when I look back at the projects, they were meaningless! How could I get so wrapped up? Now it seems like another world. I look back and just scratch my head. But when I was there, everything seemed critical!"

The pressure to respond to business opportunities is creating rapid change and high-stress work situations. IBM recently closed its sales and branch locations and employees moved home to work on their computers, faxes, and modems. *Forbes* 500 companies have experienced a 10 percent decline in employment over the past ten years. Survivors of job layoffs worry and wonder if and when they will be next. We live on the edge of constant change.

Why We Must Change

To respond rapidly to changes in our organizations and marketplaces, we must fundamentally change the way we work together.

Our typical ways of relating to each other and getting work done are as outdated and ineffective as the technologies of yesterday. They still work—just like our old typewriters still work—but they are no longer adequate to respond to the challenges we face.

Organizational structures that used to provide order, establish priorities, and set direction no longer do. Traditionally, we had a boss whom we reported to, and he or she reported to someone else. If we didn't know what to do, we asked for direction. And as long as we looked busy, no one bothered us.

Today, the boss is never there, departmental lines are fuzzy, and employees are expected to move in and out of project teams based on the needs of the business. The workplace is more fluid, functional resources are shared, and greater portions of the work are contracted to outside vendors. Emerging organizational structures are much more chaotic and unorganized than any of us would like.

Rapidly changing business conditions and uncertainty create great fear and anxiety inside of us. We are worried about losing jobs, customers, opportunities, promotions, resources, and time. We don't know what will happen if the new product fails, the legislature cuts our funding, a merger puts us out of business, or competitors underprice us in the marketplace.

Symptoms of Corporate Craziness

Without our connections to each other, it is easy to feel alone, that there is little we can do. As one venture manager said to me, "Every night I go home scared to death. I don't know if this new venture will make it. I'm afraid to tell my people. Around them I demonstrate confidence and a sense of assurance that I don't feel inside." Organizational craziness is nothing less than terror in action. It is manic, anxious behavior caused by our fears. When one person catches it—especially at the top—it spreads throughout the organization. Rather than calm ourselves, we reflect each other's anxieties and keep the frenzy alive.

Lack of Focus

One symptom of corporate craziness is the *inability to focus on one thing long enough to get it done.* We go from project to project, meeting to meeting, scattered and barely attentive—leaving loose ends, miscommunication, and confusion in our wake. There is never enough time. Weeks go by in a blur of activity. We can't distinguish one day from the next. Everything is urgent. The pressure never lets up. There is always a crisis that needs our attention. We may feel energized, but we are tightly wound, unable to settle down and consider implications and consequences.

We collect more and more balls to juggle and pride ourselves on the number we can keep in the air. An executive was asked by an exhausted group of employees to prioritize an overwhelming list of 550 initiatives. He refused, saying, "Everything is important. If I make a few my top priorities, the others won't get done." We compete with each other for resources to meet conflicting priorities, feel overwhelmed by the amount of work there is to do, and rarely experience the satisfaction of seeing a project done well. To keep up, we delegate more responsibility to others, yet we don't take time to explain what we need. We don't have time to talk. We don't have time for our personal lives: Spouses, families, and friends become intrusions on our busy schedules. Our attention is on deadlines, and deadlines are poor indicators of the real priorities.

Misuse of Technology

Technology further enables us to act out the craziness. At one company, every manager is required to carry a beeper. Ed, a program manager, describes the tension he feels eating lunch, driving home from work, or writing at his desk—always alert to the beeper that might go off. In one management meeting, there are so many beepers going off, they decide to purchase beepers that vibrate instead of make noise.

A sales manager, Jessie, describes talking to Don, one of her peers, on his car phone. During their conversation Don puts her on hold four times to answer incoming calls. Finally, he asks Jessie to hang up because he is receiving a fax on his car fax machine. Don bases his importance on the number of phone calls he receives, meetings on his calendar, and people waiting in line to see him. For him there is little time to plan, write, celebrate, learn, or reflect.

Too Busy to Care

Once I was looking for Al, a faculty member at a large university. I couldn't find him so I dropped into an office and asked if they knew where we was. No, they said they had never heard of Al— perhaps he was on a different floor. I started to take the elevator when I noticed the sign for Al's office right next to this office. He worked less than twenty feet away yet no one in this department even knew he existed, much less where his office was.

Our offices are filled with voice mail, E-mail, and computers. They are also filled with people working under the same roof, for the same institutions, who don't know each other's names. This is corporate craziness. We are too busy to care.

Organizational Depression

We can exist in a state of frenetic activity only for so long. After a time we become immune to the crises. Frenetic organizations become depressed organizations. Layoffs, restructuring, changing business strategies, and rotating jobs have left us numb, depressed, and silently discontent. We feel whipsawed by the rapid changes and no longer want to play. In depressed organizations employees express little enthusiasm. Vitality is lacking. New programs do not excite people, and motivation speeches no longer overcome the skepticism. Beneath the surface employees feel, "What's the use? Nothing is going to change. Why bother?"

What impact does all this have on our self-esteem? Work environments directly affect how we feel about ourselves. We lose confidence, overwork to prove our value, become afraid to take the initiative, and doubt the importance of our contributions. Our feelings of self-worth are difficult to separate from the way we are treated. Performance affects our self-esteem and self-esteem affects our performance. It's a circular system, one impacting the other.

Finding a Way Out of the Craziness

It is easier to catch the craziness than to find a different way to work together. We elect to play the game that is being played: We try to fit in, feel accepted, and avoid rocking the boat to get ahead even though a small voice inside us says, "This is nuts!" It takes great courage to do things differently. We have become used to the craziness. It is what we know. It is what everyone else is doing. We don't believe it can ever be different. When we slow down we feel the panic and fear that is just beneath the surface. And behind our frenetic behavior is fear. We attend to other people, data, structures, activities, and interactions to reduce our fear.

The keys to reducing frenetic activity and succeeding in the future are present in our organizations today yet greatly undervalued. In order to be successful, we must:

1. Agree on desired outcomes
2. Improve the quality of our relationships

Agreeing on Desired Outcomes

We need to focus more on outcomes than activities. We must reach agreement about what needs to be done. Activities do not always lead to results.

A benefits department follows a detailed list of procedures to administer claims. Despite incredible accuracy in following the procedures, claims are frequently paid late and customer cancellations are up by 20 percent. In another case, a group of professionals in a department of education meet to discuss their objectives. It becomes clear that each person is pursuing his or her own projects but no one has an overall vision for the department. Without coordination, planning, and agreement, the sum of the parts frequently does not add up to a whole.

The following assumptions keep us activity-driven:

- If we are not "doing something," nothing is happening.
- We don't have the luxury to sit, think, and talk.

- There are those who "think" and those who "get things done."
- If we don't do it, it won't get done.
- It's what we *do* that really counts.

We believe that if we just do something, everything will be OK. Some managers deliberately delegate the same task to more than one person to make sure it gets done. The truth is that we frequently race off to do things that don't need to be done or that someone else is already doing.

Relying on Trust, Not Control

Because activities are visible, they offer us the illusion of progress. A new sales manager asks his staff to be in the office by 7:00 A.M. He also calls meetings at the end of the day and expects everyone to attend. Wendy, the highest-performing sales professional, has a young child at home and knows how to be highly productive without putting in excessive hours. After a month of working for the new manager, she tells him she cannot meet his expectations because it means leaving her house at 6:30 A.M. and frequently not getting home until after 7:30 P.M., which leaves her little time for a personal life or time with her child. Despite Wendy's performance and sterling track record, the manager tells her she is "not cut out for the job." This manager has an activity focus, not an outcome focus, and consequently he loses a valuable contributor.

Becoming outcome-focused requires that we *trust rather than control* others. We don't prescribe how to achieve the desired outcomes. Instead, we agree on what needs to be done and allow individuals the freedom to collaborate and initiate solutions.

Focusing on outcomes allows people to create innovative ways to reach their goals. One day over lunch, Joe, a seasoned manager, describes how he changed his management style from control to an outcome focus. Picking up a cup from the table, he says,

> I used to say, "We need to move this cup from here to here," and then I would pick up the cup and move it. Now I say, "We need to move this cup from here to here.

What is the most effective way we can do this?" Now, we are collaborating and finding innovative ways to get things done better and faster.

Defining Outcomes

The following ideas are concrete ways to define outcomes before launching into action:

- When a project is starting, counter the tendency to discuss solutions before the problem is fully understood. Frequently say, "Let's understand the problem first before we talk about the solutions."
- Appoint someone as a monitor to keep the discussion from detouring prematurely into solutions or how-tos.
- Often ask, "What are we trying to achieve?" "What is the purpose of this meeting, project, or event?" and "What outcomes do we want?"
- When solutions are proposed, ask, "Will this solution prevent the problem from happening again?" If not, keep exploring the problem.
- When discussing outcomes, be specific: "When we have reached our goal, what will the results look like?" For example, if you want higher morale, ask, "How will people actually behave when we have higher morale?"
- Be sure that everyone understands and agrees upon the outcomes defined. Say, for example, "Let's talk about what we actually mean when we say 'higher profits.'"
- Use questions that encourage discussion and dialogue about objectives. Replace "Do you understand our objectives?" with "What questions or comments do you have about our objectives?"

Improving the Quality of Our Relationships

Today the quality of our relationships is as important to business success as the quality of our products and services. We need to give this area as much attention and energy as we do customer complaints, marketing strategies, and production schedules.

Improving the quality of our relationships requires that we talk openly about our expectations and disappointments and be specific about what we want and need from each other. Unspoken assumptions lead to unmet expectations and resentment. To enhance the quality of our relationships, we need to ask each other:

- How well are we getting along?
- Are we communicating effectively?
- Do others know what we want from them?
- Are we receiving what we need?
- Do we feel appreciated and valued?

These are areas we are uncomfortable discussing and often avoid. All we can imagine is wasting a colossal amount of time. Yet the answers are powerful indicators of our ability to get work done.

We can improve the quality of our daily interactions in several specific ways. At the beginning of new projects we can identify the expectations we have of each other. Many groups create up-front agreements or contracts about their working relationship. The agreements might look something like this:

- We agree to encourage honesty and candid comments.
- Regular attendance at meetings is expected.
- We will be respectful when differences arise.
- Conflicts are not discussed outside the team.
- We will celebrate our progress.

Periodically, the group or team members should revisit their agreements to add, change, or discuss how well they are meeting their expectations.

The Importance of Values

The quality of our relationships is directly affected by the values we hold. Our values determine whether we behave in ways that create trust, teamwork, quality, and customer satisfaction.

The recent surge of management interest in values indicates growing awareness of their importance. Many organizations are defining their core values and communicating them to employees. Others involve employees directly in the development of company values. Every organization needs to specify its values. *An organization without values is like a relationship without agreements.* The values that shape our relationships develop whether we talk about them or not, but they may not be acceptable to the people involved. Values offer the following benefits. They:

- Articulate what is important.
- Define the way we work together.
- Let people know what to expect.
- Communicate what is not acceptable.

Value statements encourage specific behaviors in daily work interaction. Here are some examples of value statements:

- We respect and utilize the diverse talents of individuals.
- We work collaboratively to meet customer needs.
- We act with integrity in all business decisions.
- We empower people to take initiative and make decisions.
- We recognize and acknowledge outstanding performance.
- We develop high-trust relationships with customers and each other.

Often value statements are supported by specific behaviors and attitudes, as illustrated below:

Value Statement

We develop high-trust relationships with customers and each other.

Behaviors and Attitudes That Support This Statement

- We make customers our number one priority.
- We clarify what the customer wants and needs early.

- We resolve differences that impact customer satisfaction.
- We team across departments to deliver quality services on time.

Implementing Values

Once developed, values need to be communicated and understood by every member of the organization. They need to become a living document rather than a plaque on the wall. When they are a true part of the organization, all employees are familiar with the values, and new employees learn about them on or before arrival. The values are reviewed, revised, and actively discussed because they are felt to be important. Employees expect feedback when their behavior is not consistent with the values. The questions "How do we implement our values in this situation?" and "What is the right thing to do based on our values?" are asked. Frequent stories are told about ways the values are implemented. Recognition is given when there are exemplary demonstrations of the values in action.

Actually living the values makes them come alive. But this is not always easy to do. Hewlett-Packard's value of stable employment has been put to the test many times. During periods of slow business, Hewlett-Packard management turned down lucrative military contracts because they did not provide employment security. A consumer products company reduced its oversized personnel manual to five pages of principles that managers use as guidelines to make decisions about personnel policies.

Even when we live the values, we are not immune to external changes that threaten organizational security. This can be discouraging. Shortly after several companies won the Malcolm Baldrige National Quality Award, they found themselves on the brink of financial disaster. Employees in these organizations asked, "Why should we bother trying to do things right? We are no better off than the cutthroat business down the street. We get hit with layoffs and the bottom falls out of our business." Staying true to our values when things get tough requires real commitment. Rocky roads in business are the acid test of our values. It's one thing to adhere to teamwork, trust, integrity, and collaboration when business is profitable, but it's more important to stick by them when the results are not there.

Do the Values Fit?

As organizations learn to identify and live their values, it will be easier for individuals to know if they fit in with the organization. To work daily in an environment that does not value what you value is difficult. Organizational fit with individual values is sometimes hard to achieve fully.

Yvette is the manager of a marketing department. She values direct, honest communication and hates political intrigue and favoritism. Yet she works in an organization that is full of indirect communication, where decisions are made by only a few people and confrontation is rare. Yvette's work environment conflicts with her personal values. For several years she challenges and confronts the way decisions are made and fights for the behaviors she believes are right. But nothing changes and she receives little support for her efforts. After a while she develops tension in her jaw, high blood pressure, and physical aches and pains. The environment in which she is working is toxic to her. She has one set of values and the organization has another. She realizes she will never win the battles she is fighting and her efforts are anything but appreciated. In the end she decides to leave the organization. The clearer the values, the quicker we know if the organization is right for us, and vice versa.

Comparing Values With Reality

Sometimes written values are in stark contrast with what people actually experience. If the organization's "real" values were outlined, they might look more like these:

- We value profits over people.
- We value quotas over quality.
- Always look out for number one.
- Team performance is not rewarded.
- If your opinion differs from that of the people in power, keep it to yourself.

When stated values are inconsistent with reality, they quickly lose their power and credibility. Employees think, "Wait a minute—this morning you said quality was important and now you are asking me to ship this defective product!" We do not believe what we hear: *We believe what we see and experience.*

Honesty is required to implement our values successfully. After defining the values we want in our working relationships, we need to assess current reality and what people perceive as really going on. To identify attitudes and behaviors that conflict with ideal values, ask these questions:

- What behaviors are in conflict with our stated values?
- What attitudes undermine our values?
- What expectations and norms are in conflict with our values?

Promoting values without acknowledging current reality is analogous to putting frosting on top of worms. It looks good, smells good, is appealing and inviting—but just beneath the surface is a whole different story. We are appalled at the very thought. Company values overlaying mistrust and inequities are equally distasteful. Only by accepting the perceptions that exist can decisions be made to act differently.

In the assessment of value practices, first look for broad categories of discrepancies. Then identify specific behaviors and attitudes that you can do something about. These are the findings of one company that completed this exercise of determining what behaviors were in conflict with its values.

Effective Leadership

- We have not communicated a clear direction to the organization.
- We do not follow though on the decisions we make.

We Are All in This Together

- We have no team award or recognition, only individual recognition.

- There is no orientation for new employees.
- We stay inside our functions too much.

Partnering With the Customer

- Our technical experts have poor collaboration skills with customers.
- We wait until there is a problem to initiate customer contact.

Honest Communication

- Too often we do what is expected and don't challenge current practices.

Organizations that define their values and address inconsistencies are way ahead of those that stop after the value definition stage. Managers in one company that completed an assessment made the following changes to implement their values:

- They changed its compensation system to reward team performance.
- They improved follow-through on decisions.
- They trained technical personnel in customer skills.

The benefit of honest assessment and follow-through is increased buy-in and commitment to the values by all employees.

Stopping Corporate Craziness

Corporate craziness is symptomatic of our inability to work well together. In the old model we competed to get ahead, protected our budgets, and filled our departments with all the head counts we could justify. This behavior no longer suits us or the needs of our organizations. Just underneath the surface of our behavior is fear and uncertainty about the changes that assail us. Our fears and inability to work together cost us far more than any external threat.

The new bottom line in business is that we need each other. To stop the craziness, we must listen and talk about what is on our minds.

Complex solutions and fast time-to-market can be achieved only through clarity of vision and effective collaboration. We need agreement on outcomes, innovative solutions, and successful implementation. We can no longer wait for decisions from on high. No one person, group, or program has the answers. Smart decisions and profitable initiatives require input from many sources, calm discussion of implications, adequate time to plan, and trust that allows us to implement.

ACTION EXERCISES

Exercise 1: Identifying Symptoms of Corporate Craziness

The purpose of this exercise is to identify and discuss corporate craziness and changes you can make individually or as a group to improve effectiveness.

1. Check the following symptoms of craziness that you observe in your organization, and discuss them:

   ____ Lack of focus or direction
   ____ Frenetic behaviors
   ____ Obsession with technology
   ____ Too busy working to care
   ____ Depression or attitude of not caring
   ____ Crisis-orientation
   ____ Judgmental attitudes
   ____ Secretiveness about decisions
   ____ Indirect or vague communication
   ____ Intolerance for mistakes
   ____ Excessive number of closed-door conversations

2. Note the following ways you participate in the craziness:

   - What I do that doesn't make sense is . . .
   - If I were brave, I would stop doing . . .
   - I question the effectiveness of the following activities but do them anyway:

3. Decide on immediate changes you can make to improve effectiveness:

   - I can stop doing . . .
   - I can better understand why . . .
   - I can improve the way we . . .

Exercise 2: Defining Workplace Values

The purpose of this exercise is to develop value statements and bring current practices in line with the values.

1. Ask individuals in a group to write on note cards or Post-it Notes specific behaviors that are important to the success of your

organization. Write one behavior on each card. Make sure that each statement includes a verb. For example, "We respect each other's abilities" and "We collaborate with customers."
2. Collect the cards and group them into similar categories. Give each category a heading.
3. Summarize and refine the value and behavioral statements until they express what you aspire to do.
4. In a second meeting, review your actual behaviors and values and find discrepancies. Then make a list of attitudes and behaviors that do not support the values. Be gentle but honest with each other.
5. To take action, prioritize the behaviors you want to change and commit to one to three individual changes.
6. To sustain commitment, meet in three months and again in six months to assess how well you are doing.

Exercise 3: Improving Work Relationships

The purpose of this exercise is to ensure the effectiveness of your working relationships. Don't wait for problems to arise. Use the following questions to communicate and improve how well you are working together.

1. Ask how well you are working together to:

   - Set goals clearly
   - Understand each other's point of view
   - Express appreciation
   - Utilize each other's skills and talents
   - Communicate what you need
   - Make decisions
   - Follow through on decisions

2. At the end of meetings and projects, ask these questions:

   - What is working well?
   - What needs to be improved?

3. At the beginning of working sessions, take time to discuss thoughts, questions, or feelings about how you are doing as a team or concern you have about the project.

7

The Changing Relationship Between Managers and Employees

If you cannot get rid of the family skeleton, you may as well make it dance.

—George Bernard Shaw, British playwright

Tim, the purchasing manager, is frustrated. He turns to Rhonda, one of his employees, for help with a problem.

Tim: Rhonda, please take this form back to engineering and get them to indicate the quantity they want. We may be geniuses in purchasing but we aren't mind readers!

Rhonda: Tim, engineering already told us how much they want. It's stated on their initial request. This is just a follow-up notice.

Tim: Why isn't the quantity indicated on *this* form? We've always asked them to write that information on both forms.

Rhonda: Our improvement team decided it was better to ask departments to complete only one form. That way depart-

ments don't get frustrated by duplicate forms and we
end up with fewer errors because we have only one
place to check.

Tim: But how will I know the quantity they want?

Rhonda: You have to check the original request. All the data you
need is on that form.

Tim: Does that mean I no longer see the quantity on *this* form?

Rhonda: That's right.

Tim: I don't like this! I want this form changed back to the
way it used to be! This is very inconvenient.

Rhonda: But you asked us to improve the process, and this is
what we came up with.

Tim: Well, I don't like it!

The New Structure of Manager/Employee Relationships

This dialogue highlights the conflicts that can arise as managers
and employees move from traditional structures into new, participative structures. To respond quickly and more intelligently to the
marketplace, managers are now empowering individuals, using
teams, and moving away from authoritarian practices into coaching and facilitating behaviors. Employees are leaving isolated,
functional responsibilities and compliance behaviors and moving
into teaming roles and matrixed decision making. The accompany-
ing diagram summarizes the difference between traditional and
newly emerging structures. See Figure 5.

In the new structure, roles are often ambiguous and uncertain.
Former attitudes and behaviors are no longer appropriate, but new
practices are not well understood. Managers ask:

"Am I giving up too much control?

"How do I hold people accountable?"

"How do I make sure the work gets done with so many employees working on teams outside the department?

"How do I handle performance issues in an empowered culture?"

"When do I, as a manager, get to say no?"

Figure 5. Traditional vs. new structures.

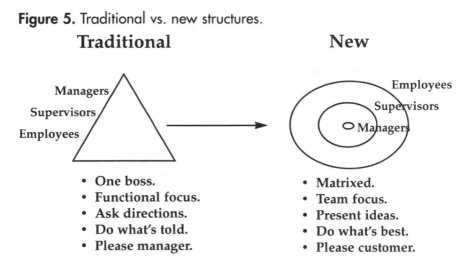

Traditional   # New

- One boss.
- Functional focus.
- Ask directions.
- Do what's told.
- Please manager.

- Matrixed.
- Team focus.
- Present ideas.
- Do what's best.
- Please customer.

Employees have their own set of questions about their new role:

"How much empowerment do I really have?"

"When do I need to get permission for a decision from my manager?"

"What happens if the team decides one thing and the manager disagrees?"

"The company is promoting teams but my manager doesn't want me to work on a team. What am I supposed to do?"

Radical changes in the roles have made our relationships with each other tenuous. Managers and employees dance around each other, unsure of what to expect. We move forward hesitantly, afraid to break with traditional codes of conduct yet unable to proceed without fully doing so! Employees wonder, "When will the ax fall?" And managers speculate, "Is this really going to work?"

Under the old rules, differences and conflicts were less likely to emerge. And if they did, we knew who was going to win. There weren't as many opportunities for relationships to get out of whack. Today, communications are full of mixed messages. One minute employees hear, "You are empowered," and the next, "Do what you're told." The new roles are neither defined nor unanimously accepted. Under these conditions, misunderstandings and conflicts are bound to arise. The following are a list of frustrations managers in the new work environment experience with employees:

• The employee is passive, lacks initiative, and acts like a victim.

> "I can't do this. I'm not capable."
> "I only do what you tell me to do."
> "I wish you would do something about this."

• The employee feels entitled or blames others for his or her problems.

> "It's my right to have this job."
> "It's all their fault."
> "If only management would fix this."

• The employee is competitive with others and too independent.

> "I want all the good projects."
> "I can do it myself and I don't need to work with others."
> "I don't want you telling me what to do."

Managers must address these behaviors in order to develop employees and improve work performance.

Employees are also frustrated by their managers' behaviors. Here are common employee complaints:

• The manager is too authoritarian and protective.

> "If I say 'make it happen,' it better happen."
> "Keeping employees off guard keeps them in line."
> "This is my department, my people. Stay out!"

• The manager is gone, distant in behavior, or won't make a decision.

> "I can't be human or get close to my people."
> "I have no time for employee concerns."
> "I must get agreement from everyone before I decide."

- The manager is too controlling and policy-driven.

  "I treat everyone the same."
  "I want to know everything that is going on."
  "I need to make all the decisions myself."

Sometimes manager/employee tensions manifest like a low-grade infection. At other times they erupt as full-blown communicable diseases.

In our new roles, the biggest question becomes: *How do we resolve our differences?* No one quite knows how to address missed expectations, disagreements, and authority issues. We have lost our underpinnings. All we can imagine is reverting to what we used to do—which is no longer appropriate or effective.

Unraveling the Issues: The Underlying Dynamics

To address conflicts, we must go beyond the behavioral symptoms and look at the underlying dynamics. Beneath the surface we find long-standing expectations and assumptions that keep our current behaviors in place.

Organizations are environments where the early dynamics of family relationships are played out. We carry traditional role expectations of "Mom," "Dad," and "children" into manager/employee relationships. At work, managers are expected to play the role of parents—the people who do what's right, take care of the kids, and make the right decisions. Employees are expected to play the role of children—obedient and respectful to parents and in need of protection, nurturing, and development.

These purely archetypal roles are useful if we don't take them literally to imply that employees are children and managers are parents, but rather use them to help us understand the inherent, underlying expectations that exist just beneath the surface of reporting relationships. Referencing family expectations makes it easier for us to grasp the assumptions that cause conflict in manager/employee relationships.

For our purposes in understanding manager/employee dynamics, *parent* implies an individual in an authority position, *Dad* refers to the decision-making, authority role, *Mom* to the nurturing, caregiver role, and *child* to an individual in a dependent position. Any role can be played by a man or woman. What determines the role is the individual's position in relationship to the other person and the type of power and authority he or she has.

Expectations and Assumptions

Let's consider the basic assumptions we have about family life. The expected role of the parents is to help the child grow so that one day he or she can become a responsible adult. We believe that parents should be respected and that children should be treated fairly. We don't encourage favoring of one child over the others. We realize that when the parents fight, the children often get caught in the middle. We recognize that it is good for the parents to have time for themselves. We know that abusive, permissive, and overcontrolling parents create unhealthy environments for children. And we recognize that some parents are better than others.

We may replace the word *parents* with the word *managers*, but we have much the same situation. The same type of dynamics that exist in families also exists in our organizations. Regardless of the fact that employees are grown adults, they are in the dependent role.

Managers have the responsibility of caring for and directing employee work activities, and employees have the responsibility of learning, producing, and working in cooperation with their peers. Employees are acutely aware of their managers' behavior and want to please them. They learn to read the cues, quickly note any favoritism, and become experts at anticipating their managers' needs.

The Importance of Relationships at the Top

Just as the relationship between Mom and Dad affects the kids, the relationship between the primary leaders has a significant impact on the level of cooperation among employees.

Will, the president of a bank, prefers to work on external issues and expects his operations manager, Brian, to run the day-today business. However, Brian and Will do not respect each other's abilities. Each sees the other as deficient in some way.

To deal with their differences, they agree to stay out of each other's area of responsibility. Their relationship is like that of a married couple who share the same house but sleep in separate bedrooms. Brian and Will's solution solves their interpersonal problems, but the organization as a whole suffers. Will's new ideas and strategic perspectives do not become incorporated, and the business is managed from a tactical perspective. The bank is very profitable in the short term, but over the long term, it fails to adapt to the changing marketplace. The heart of the problem in this organization is the breakdown between the president and the operations manager. Basically, the "parents" don't communicate, so the whole family suffers.

Whenever a group of individuals or departments are not getting along, always look up and you will probably find the same tensions one level up, only among fewer people. The conflicts may be very subtle, but nevertheless employees act them out! Often, the best solution to employee conflicts is first to address the issues that exist among their managers, then address the employees' issues. At this point, many of the problems will have magically disappeared.

It's especially important to solve problems between managers because when their managers fight or compete, employees act out. Managers assume they have an employee problem when in reality they have a management problem. When leaders are not cooperating, business priorities are not clear, and employees receive mixed messages and feel emotionally pulled to take sides. In these situations, some employees will "play one parent against the other" and use the loss of authority by one person to get their way.

Harry, a strong-willed employee, ignores his supervisor, Sally. He goes directly to the department manager, Len, to ask for direction and advice. Harry complains to Len about Sally's ineptness as a supervisor and asks him to do something about it. Silently, Len agrees with many of Harry's comments, but he has never spoken to Sally about them. Len gives Harry a sympathetic ear and then asks Sally to "handle Harry" so he will stop complaining to him.

Len does not realize that it is his own behavior that is undermining Sally's performance as a manager.

The real solution comes when Len and Sally discuss their relationship. After they reach agreement on what they need from each other, they are able to discuss the issues that Harry wants addressed. When Sally and Len improve their relationship, they not only provide Harry with solutions, they also create a better working situation for him.

Sibling Rivalry

Just as brothers and sisters fight and compete with each other, so do individuals in organizations—often to get the attention of their superiors! A standard practice in many companies is for the CEO to set up competition among the staff to see who will replace him or her. For a long time this practice was considered good management, when in reality it breaks down the cooperation that is essential to solving problems and leading an organization.

Competition is one of the most detrimental behaviors in our organizations. Managers and employees compete for higher positions, more status, bigger budgets, better bonuses, and greater power and control. Competition leads to withholding information, undermining, backbiting, and lack of cooperation for fear it will give the other group or person the advantage. In highly competitive environments, people work for their own advancement and not for the good of the organization and its customers. Sometimes the behavior of managers and employees makes it hard to believe they work for the same company! Internal rivalry needs to be recognized and resolved because it detracts enormous energy from the real competitors.

The Problem of Inept Managers

Just as there are adults who should not be parents, there are individuals who should not manage people. When employees repeatedly act out, want to change managers, threaten lawsuits, or have morale issues, sometimes the problem is the manager.

Unhealthy Management Behaviors

Three types of unhealthy behaviors indicate that managers have problems:

1. Abusive behavior
2. Permissive behavior
3. Controlling behavior

Abusive Behavior

Like abusive parents, abusive managers use their power in ways that are emotionally damaging to employees' well-being. Barry, a high-level vice president in an electrical company, is well known in the company for his abusive treatment. When someone makes what Barry considers a mistake, he calls the person into his office and verbally abuses him or her. He rants, yells, and shames the person for his or her behaviors. Barry's indictments can last from thirty minutes to over two hours, depending upon the stamina of the person and whether he or she breaks down before he is through. At the end of the session, the person is sent back to work. Everyone knows when the meetings are happening. But no one steps in to stop or question Barry's abusive behavior toward employees.

Just as we often do not question emotionally abusive parents unless there are physical symptoms, neither do we question repeated, abusive behavior from specific managers. The rule is: *Never interfere in the relationship between boss and employee.* The human resources manager may discuss the issue with Barry, but he or she is basically powerless to take action unless someone higher up is supportive of a change. More often than not, nothing will happen. As long as the manager makes the bottom line, we stay out of the way, silently condoning the behavior. Barry is one of the highest-paid officials in the company—yet his behavior is abusive.

At work, emotional abuse can be as devastating as physical abuse. Abusive behavior happens every day and goes unchecked in organizations. Angry, insecure managers are intimidating people who dare not fight back.

Permissive Behavior

Like overly permissive parents, permissive managers do as much if not more damage to employees than abusive managers. Permissive managers let the ship steer itself. They are afraid to take the helm and ultimately frustrate everyone who reports to them. One such manager accepts an appointment as commissioner of a state agency. She does not like conflict and avoids disagreements at all cost. When employees come to her with their ideas, she approves them all. But when a project receives heavy public criticism, she supports the public view, denies her involvement in the project, and lets the staff person hang out to dry. In addition, decisions aren't made, internal personnel issues run rampant, and projects stall because there is no focus, leadership, or support. Several employees take advantage of the situation, spending money differently than is appropriated and meeting with legislative staff to undermine projects being initiated by their peers.

The ability to take a stand, make decisions, and address conflicts is central to the role of management. Most of us are anything but experts in these areas because they are difficult and require a high level of interpersonal skill. However, there are individuals whose very essence crumbles when they are faced with any type of conflict. They may be excellent speakers, promoters, or technical experts, but they should not be in management positions that force them to make decisions and deal with conflicts and interpersonal issues.

Controlling Behavior

Just as certain parents overcontrol their children and don't let them make mistakes, certain managers overcontrol their people and keep them from developing. Jane manages an administrative department for an insurance company. Her people are extremely unhappy as they describe their work situation:

> Jane treats us like babies. We have been doing this work for over five years, and we still have to go to her for all decisions. We are like peons waiting for her to tell us what to do next. The only work we do on our own is manual input and running reports. Even an idiot can get those right.

Jane is an overly controlling manager who is not developing her people. Her employees' distress is shouting at her to develop them. But Jane's talents, interests, and ability to contribute reside in her technical expertise. No one is going to train Iris to be a good people developer—it is simply not an area that she is interested in. Ideally, Jane would be a respected technical consultant to line management and not a manager of people.

Changing the Status of Managers

Not everyone wants to manage, cares about people, is interested in learning the skills, or finds any satisfaction in the job of management. Yet in our organizations, it is almost impossible to gain status of any kind without becoming a manager. If you are not a manager, you are not considered a serious player. The current value we place on being a manager is so highly institutionalized that it will take extraordinary measures and revolutionary new attitudes to release ourselves from this mind-set.

Our priorities are in the wrong place. There are outstanding leaders, motivators, and technical experts who should be in significant positions in the organization and *completely free from the job of managing people so they can contribute their real talents.* We need to make people management a specialized skill that not everyone has to do in order to gain a position of importance.

The people we put in management positions need to be exceptional coaches—managers who know how to work with many types of people and bring out the best in them. Employees say about these managers, "Jerry has a way of always making you want to do your best. I always know he cares about each of us. I never want to let him down. I'll never forget the team spirit and what we are able to do under his leadership." People always remember how it feels to be managed by someone who believes in them and encourages them. Xerox, a company with an excellent reputation for people management, expects individuals to demonstrate competency in team leadership and people skills before they are placed in management positions.

The New Role of Management

The new role of management is to help employees get ready to fly and to encourage them once they're off. Without being overly protective, managers should find ways to support and encourage employee development. Specifically, managers can:

- Develop people who can contribute to the whole—not just their part.
- Orient employees to the values of the company.
- Create environments where people can tell the truth.
- Teach others their job so they can move on.

In the new organization, we make sure that employees have in-depth knowledge of the business and know the critical issues. We encourage them to learn about other functions so they have a bigger perspective on the work they are doing. We provide important information—formerly locked up in files or in our heads. When a project or team requires employees to spend time in another department, we encourage them to do so. We make sure that they know the value of serving the customer and that they see us walking our talk.

We trust employees until they show us we can't. If there are performance issues, we address them immediately. We assume employees are responsible adults and respond to their requests for help. We spend time talking to them and getting to know the issues they face so that when they come to us for help, we understand their situation and can help solve the problem. We build a team and encourage individuals to trust and rely upon each other. When employee tensions arise, we encourage them to speak directly to each other and work things out.

The New Role of Employees

As the role of management changes, so does the role of employees. When children grow up, they sometimes don't want to leave home. Growing up is wonderful and frightening at the same time. In the same way, some employees will resist the change. New behaviors are risky. The employees who do initiate new behaviors will feel, "It's my job that's on the line—not the manager's. I'm the one taking the risk, stepping up to the challenge, and sticking my neck out." After all, when the mother bird kicks the babies out of the nest, it's the babies who have to fly! And flying is terrifying.

Some employees want to fly and others don't. Not all will be ready at the same time. Many would rather watch to see what happens when the first ones step over the edge. Will the others be supported, and how well will they survive? If it looks safe, then they might try too. It is critical what happens to the early risk takers who sign up for teams, work outside their departments, talk to higher level managers, and initiate procedures that serve the customer. If they get beaten up, punished, fired, displaced, or criticized by management, no one else will follow their lead. And why should they?

Employees need to walk though the door to decision making, increased responsibility, and confidential information as managers open it. The act of walking through this door needs to be respected because it means more than accepting responsibility. It means fundamentally changing the nature of employees' relationship to management. The supervisor is no longer responsible and to blame. All the things you always wanted to try but "they said you couldn't" become possibilities to explore. The old rules that someone else enforced must now be examined to see if they make any sense. *Us* versus *them* is a game of the past. Now, instead of blaming others, we seek information. When we need something, we ask for it. When we see something wrong, we talk about it. When we want something to be different, we take action. And we don't do it alone. We realize that managers have information and perspectives that we need. We accept that our actions have implications for others, and we get buy-in and commitment before blazing ahead. Blind obedience is replaced with curiosity; compliance is replaced with initiative. Becoming responsible means looking our old job in the face and seeing all the ways it didn't work and could be better. We know what needs to get done, and we take the responsibility for doing it.

Resolving Our Differences

Our organizations are far from this vision and we know it. The changes we need will not happen overnight. It will take whole groups of people working consistently in new ways to change the dominant culture. In the meantime, how do we address the issues and differences that come up? When manager/employee relationships break down and unmet expectations and misunderstandings surface, how do we resolve these problems in a new way? Although uncomfortable, these troublesome situations are the new classrooms that can help us identify our needs and develop the skills we are missing. These conflicts provide us with the opportunity to move beyond our current level of understanding and experience.

There are three steps to the process of resolving our differences:

1. Seek level ground.
2. Look at the task.
3. Make it up.

Step One: Seeking Level Ground

The first step of resolving our differences is to *seek level ground*. We will get nowhere if we continue to stay in our one-up, one-down positions. To begin a new way of working together, we must agree to start on equal footing. This means saying, "Your needs are as important as mine. I am interested in your point of view and I want you to hear mine."

The biggest question that employees have at this point is: "If I open up and share my opinions and feelings, will there be punishment?" This is a valid question and deserves an honest answer from management before any discussion is started. Managers should:

- Begin by finding ways to neutralize fear. Set up the meeting in a neutral location—not your office or theirs.

  - Talk about expectations for the conversation. Say:

    "Your needs are as important as my needs."
    "I am interested in your point of view and I want you to hear mine."
    "I would like us to talk openly with each other."
    "What questions do you have or reassurances do you need to speak openly?"

- Describe the incident/behavior that concerns you. Listen to their point of view, then summarize both points of view. (Do not problem solve at this time.)

From an equal position, we need to start talking about how we feel about our relationship with each other:

"You hurt me when you did this."
"I don't like it when you . . . ."
"In the meeting, you gave Jan the assignment that I thought was mine and I felt . . . . "

The talking continues until each side has shared and listened to the other.

As we talk and listen, we need to acknowledge and forgive each other's humanness. Just as our parents did not mean to hurt us or our children to negate us, neither do we deliberately mean to hurt each other. What will help us is to talk and to understand how we hurt each other. Then we need to move on. Trying to fix or problem solve our hurts won't work. We must leave them alone and let them heal. Sharing them is enough.

Step Two: Looking at the Task

The next phase of the process is to *look at the task* and make a decision on priorities and actions needed. To do so, discuss the work at hand and agree on what needs to be done. Say:

"What is the situation in front of us?"
"What needs to be done?"
"What are the priorities?"

This portion of the process is not about the relationship but rather about the actual work you need to do together. What is important in this step is that you both agree on what you are trying to accomplish.

Step Three: Making It Up

The final step requires you to return to the relationship and make decisions about how you will work together. This step is called *making it up* because there are no longer any rules like "You are the boss so tell me what to do." In this step you have the opportunity to shed old roles and expectations that did not work and make decisions about the changes you would like to create. Hopefully, the ways you choose to interact in the future will be based on your mutual needs rather than on any prescribed set of rules.

In this step:

- Discuss and agree on the roles you want to have in the project or work at hand.
- Make decisions about behaviors and expectations of each other.
- Agree to the amount of time you will try out new behaviors.
- Set a time to follow up and agree on what's working and what's not.

It is important in this step that you make agreements that are simple and easy to implement. Give yourselves time to try out and assess the new behaviors. Continuing to touch base about how things are working is important because it helps you refine and modify as you go rather than learn everything and change it all at once.

Relating as Adults

Traditional roles of parents and children are fading as old structures evolve into new ones. We are now moving toward adult relationships with each other where teamwork and mutual respect will replace obedience to authority and compliance with rules.

What we feel when our kids grow up and are successfully on their own is a bit of nostalgia and an enormous amount of pride. We will have the same feelings about our relationships at work. As we work through our differences and learn to partner in new ways, we will feel pride in who we are becoming, in watching employees' development, and in what we are accomplishing together.

ACTION EXERCISES

Exercise 1: Identifying Changes in Roles and Expectations

The purpose of this exercise is to help you identify changes in manager/employee roles and resultant expectations and implications.

1. Review the diagram of traditional structures and new structures presented in this chapter. Then identify the changes you have seen and experienced as a manager or employee.

   In the past,
   - I was expected to:
   - My role was to:
   - How things worked was:

   Today,
   - I am expected to:
   - My role is to:
   - How things work is:

2. Identify the implication of these changes ("This means I take more risks . . . , must deal with . . . , make decisions about . . . , etc.).

Exercise 2: Understanding the Dynamics of Manager/Employee Relationships

The purpose of this exercise is to understand the underlying dynamics of manager/employee relationships and apply this understanding to your work situation. Reflect on your own situation and answer these questions:

1. How are manager/employee relationships similar to parent/child relationships?

   - Spoken similarities and expectations
   - Unspoken similarities and expectations

2. What games are similar to the dynamics in family life?

   - Sibling rivalry
   - Favoritism

- "Go ask Mom"
- "Wait till I tell Dad"

3. How does recognizing these dynamics impact your management behavior?

   - What manager/employee expectations do you want to change?
   - What behaviors can become more "adult" in nature?

8

Aligning Organizational Needs and Individual Talents

One does not discover new lands without consenting to lose sight of the shore for a very long time.

—André Gide, French novelist and critic

As organizations respond to a highly competitive marketplace, job change and insecurity become a way of life. Managers lay off employees, displace work overseas, hire outside contractors, buy and sell companies, reorganize, assign individuals to new positions, and require different skills for current jobs. Employment uncertainty has never been so high. Many of us remember when going to work for an organization was considered a lifetime commitment, and the standard expectation was internal promotion, longevity of tenure, and guaranteed employment.

Today, layoffs are happening at every level. It is not uncommon for entire divisions and companies to be eliminated. No one can expect job security. Between 1980 and 1993, employment declined in the *Forbes* 500 by 10 percent.* The 1994 Bureau of Labor

* Robert Rosenstein, "Where Did All the People Go," *Forbes*, April 25, 1994.

Statistics figures show the average college graduate will stay in a particular occupation for about eight years. By contrast, those without a high school degree will stay in one occupation for approximately five years. At my son's high school graduation this year, in sharp contrast to optimistic messages in the past, the commencement speaker bluntly told graduates they should expect to be laid off, to change careers at least three times during their working lives, and to hold ten or more jobs.

As these statistics become reality, people feel like Ping-Pong balls. And the uncertainties of change are affecting people throughout the organization. Executives feel as insecure about their positions as do front-line employees. People at all levels come to work and wonder, "Will I have a job for the rest of the year? Will I be relocated? When will my manager or job assignment change?" Externally, we are busy with work tasks, but internally, we are pondering how we will be affected by what will happen next.

New Career Opportunities

For some, the rapid changes have brought growth opportunities as the need for new products and services has accelerated.

- Judy, a sales consultant, has expanded her business into services for accountants, engineers, and lawyers who realize they must market and sell their services, not just respond to phone calls.
- Bronson, who held a rote production job, has developed the skills to be a team leader and now trains employees in factory locations across the country.
- Brenda, an administrative assistant, started learning about computers ten years ago. Today, she is overseeing the installation of a new computer system for the entire company. Her career has grown in ways she never thought possible.

To those who are able to capitalize on changing situations, the future can be exciting and profitable.

Eight Career Dilemmas

Risk and opportunity go hand in hand. The following are eight career dilemmas that individuals find themselves facing in the rapidly changing job market.

1. Need to Create Something New

Mike is a business developer who likes to start new companies, launch innovative products, and oversee acquisitions. As soon as the business or venture is successful, Mike wants to start a new company. He sometimes resents trading in the financial security he has achieved.

2. Burned Out but Afraid to Leave

Walt, a senior finance manager, experiences feelings of unrest. He thinks, "There must be more to life than this! I'd like to teach and live on a horse ranch—perhaps do something with my hands. I'm tired of working just to pay the bills. This is my life!"

3. Medical Needs Determine Job Situation

After two years with her company, Megan discovers she has a medical condition that could develop into a serious problem later in life. Megan wants to go into consulting with her husband, but she is afraid to lose her health care coverage.

4. Reputation Prevents Promotion

Ryan develops a reputation as a troublemaker when he objects to an expensive new machine that is being installed in the plant. One day his manager calls him into the office and tells him bluntly,

"Either get on the team or off of it!" Now Ryan wonders if he has any future with the company.

5. Self-Image Affects Ability to Make a Change

Karen has worked over twenty years in the same accounting firm. She is the mainstay of the company whom everyone relies on for help. Secretly, Karen wishes she could work a four-day week. She realizes that to make the change she must give up being "the responsible one who is always there."

6. Work Restricts Upward Mobility

Bud wants to move into marketing but heavy work demands require him to stay in his position far beyond the time he is ready to leave. Bud considers moving to a new company to achieve the change he desires.

7. Need for Status Prevents Right Job Fit

As a benefits administrator, Yvonne excels. But when she is promoted to benefits manager, she fails miserably. When approached with the possibility of returning to her former job, Yvonne refuses and fights to stay in her management position.

8. Fear of Making a Job Change

Bruce knows change is risky, and he doesn't want to rock the boat. He says, "Here, at least I know how things operate. If I make a change, it might not be any better. I would rather stay with what I know than take a chance."

The Need for Career Development

A great deal of work effectiveness is lost when we are in positions that are not suited to our interests and priorities. Imagine how much productivity would be achieved if our jobs were matched precisely with our talents, interests, and abilities.

Customer needs, changes in technology, and shrinking time-to-market are creating new jobs and skill development opportunities. Formerly isolated, back room employees are solving problems once handled by field people. Information experts are now facilitating customer user-groups, department managers are designing processes that revolutionize functional responsibilities, and marketing managers are moving away from databases and spending more time in the field.

But as jobs become more fluid, an increasing number of people are fearful about losing their jobs. Thus, we have greater need for job change and more fear about job loss happening at the same time. Many organizations make career development an individual matter, and only a few companies have assumed adequate responsibility for assisting employees in this area.

The benefit of this tumultuous situation is that it provides enhanced opportunities for career development and the use of individuals' talents. However, to take advantage of this opportunity, organizations must free themselves of habitual attitudes and behaviors that limit the support provided for career change. Aligning individual talents with organizational needs requires that we make it safe for individuals to address employment concerns. Specifically, we need to:

- Address performance issues.
- Change our IN versus OUT mind-set.
- Help employees get into the right jobs.
- Make it safe to address career concerns.
- Provide support for exploration.
- Encourage individuals to use their best talents.

Addressing Performance Issues

Managers frequently say that giving negative performance feedback is the most difficult part of their job. Some avoid giving feedback altogether. One such manager, Alice, spent two years supervising Beth, an employee she did not believe was technically capable of doing her job. Rather than discuss these issues with Beth, Alice avoids her, passes her up for special projects, and silently judges her work as unprofessional. Privately, she wishes Beth would find another job. Beth knows something is wrong but cannot put her finger on the problem. Lack of feedback creates an insidious environment of mistrust.

Receiving feedback is very beneficial. It helps us know how we are being perceived by others. Sometimes we are surprised by the feedback. Other times we disagree, but overall we benefit from knowing how others see us. Too frequently we dance around the issues we have with each other. We say, "That went fine," when we need to say, "Your approach in the meeting was overbearing and kept others from participating" or "The presentation did not go well because you included too many details." *Giving people feedback is a caring activity*. It means we are willing to take the time to help others improve by talking about their strengths and weaknesses.

Performance feedback tends to stop after a certain level of management, but all individuals need feedback. The higher up we go in the organization, the more people we impact by our behavior. To provide feedback high up, some companies have initiated a process called 360 Feedback where peers, employees, and bosses evaluate the effectiveness of managers and employees.

Not everyone wants to give or receive feedback. Managers are afraid of the emotional reactions that employees might have to their comments, and employees often feel threatened by feedback. Success with performance feedback requires more than compliance with annual performance reviews or the use of sophisticated forms. *It requires that we have a relationship with each other that is built on trust*. The person receiving the feedback must know we are on his or her side. Within the context of a supportive relationship, negative and positive feedback is very useful. Without this type of relationship, suggestions for improvement can generate feelings of inadequacy and shame.

Changing Our "In" vs. "Out" Mind-Set

We have an IN or OUT attitude regarding employment. When we are employed by an organization, we are considered a member of the family. If we leave, we are no longer a member. To those who are IN, we offer respect, support, and guidance, but to those who leave or are on their way OUT, we offer much less.

Never are the IN versus OUT attitudes more felt than when we leave an organization. There is a stripping down that occurs when we turn in our keys and surrender the badge that once gave us unlimited access. Yes, the reality of leaving an organization is that there are security issues, that we no longer have a role to play, and that we need to leave company property behind. However, the underlying message that is communicated in the leaving process is that we no longer belong.

The new work environment requires us to reexamine this IN vs. OUT mind-set. Old faces may reappear in new settings and may be critical to the success of our business. Former employees may return as consultants or go to work for customers, competitors, and community agencies down the street. There are benefits to protecting and nurturing our former relationships rather than discarding them. Relationships need to be honored regardless of whether or not the person works for our company anymore. When employees quit because their skills and interests no longer fit, are dismissed because the organization does not need their talents, or are laid off, we can no longer afford to turn our backs and discard them outright. We need to make it safe and easy for people to leave an organization.

Layoffs

During a layoff, the feelings of being OUT of the family are painfully obvious, especially in some companies. The former employees of one banking organization recall their layoff experience with pain. One Wednesday afternoon, seventy-five employees were told by their managers to attend a meeting at the local Holiday Inn. The executive in charge opened the session and abruptly announced, "Due to financial difficulty, we can no longer employ your services with this company. As of now you are terminated. For security reasons you are asked not to return to the office. A security guard will bring you any personal belongings you have left in the building."

The behavior of this management team told severed employees: "We no longer care about you. You are expendable. *We owe you nothing.* Your reactions and feelings are not important to us." A great deal of damage was done to the reputation of this organization as employees, families, and friends learned about and responded to the manner in which these employees were laid off.

Helping Employees Get into the Right Jobs

We need to stop rejecting people when they don't fit into our organization and help them find a place to contribute.

Doris is employed in a small company as a marketing assistant but her skills are not in this area. Her manager is constantly frustrated because the numbers Doris calculates are wrong and the reports she prepares are incomplete.

Doris is a difficult person to deal with because she has a desperate need to be important and noticed. An opportunity for Doris to contribute her talents occurs when the company decides to move to a new floor, and Doris is put in charge of the move. Immediately, she starts to excel. She oversees every detail, makes hundreds of arrangements, plans and organizes schedules with precision, and successfully orchestrates the move.

But once the move is over, Doris returns to her marketing job, and her attention-seeking behavior returns. Her manager does not know what to do. Doris has just provided a tremendous service to the company, but now the organization no longer has any need for her skills. After numerous, unsuccessful attempts at coaching Doris to do her regular marketing job, the manager fires her. Doris is devastated and leaves the office in a huff. She never wants to see anyone who works there again.

In the traditional mind-set, it is assumed that Doris would adapt to the work of the company or find a new job that met her interests. But Doris needed more help than this. From her manager, she needed (1) specific information about what she was good and not good at doing, (2) clear direction that she needed to look for this type of work in another company, and (3) encouragement, support, and strategies to find a job that matched her interests and skills. Typically, managers have not considered it their responsibility to provide this much career support to an employee, especially if the person is going to work for another organization. But until an employee is in a job that suits his or her abilities, everyone suffers: the organization, the individual, and the manager.

Making It Safe to Address Career Concerns

There are growing numbers of employees who are afraid to risk changing jobs. And too often, it is not safe to tell one's current manager about one's growing sense of boredom with the job. Verbalizing a desire to change can be synonymous with threatening our job security and position in the company.

The opposite needs to be true. Individuals considering a career change need all the help they can get from current managers and fellow employees on the best decision to make.

Fred works for a large medical company and knows from shrinking budgets and frequent layoffs that the organization is in serious trouble. He decides to nurture his latent interest in education and begins teaching business classes in the evening at a community college. At work during the day, he talks openly with managers and peers about his educational interests, future dreams, and outside work responsibilities. Six months later, Fred is laid off. He thinks to himself, "I was naive. I should never have told them." Fred's manager confides in him, "Fred, *you didn't play the game*. Talking about your career plans wasn't smart. You didn't play your cards right."

Fred has gone against the unwritten rules. He is actively making a plan for his new life and discussing his progress. Others in the organization are also in the process of making new career plans, but they are following the unwritten rules that state:

- Act as if you intend to stay with the company forever.
- Pretend this is the most important job in the world.

To behave differently is considered a betrayal to peers and to the organization. But what if these rules are wrong? What if we encourage each other to talk openly about emerging interests and assist one another in finding the best fit for our talents? Would we work less than we do now with career issues rumbling through our minds? Offering support to individuals who want to make career changes is a paradigm shift for us. It requires that we adopt the following beliefs:

- It is beneficial to discuss feelings we have about our work situation.
- It is essential to talk honestly and precisely about performance issues.
- It is a sign of growth when personal interests and priorities change.
- Organizations win when individuals are able to use their best talents.
- It is beneficial to support individuals who want to leave the organization.
- There are adequate opportunities for individual talents to be utilized.

Providing Support for Exploration

The following activities can be used to encourage career exploration:

- Encourage employees to conduct informational interviews where they talk with individuals from different departments and learn about different jobs.
- Establish job exchange programs where employees work in other areas on assignments that last a day or up to three months.
- Provide assessment and testing services that define the skills needed for different jobs and assess the person's current level

of skill before placing him or her in a specific job. Assessment programs are traditionally found in sales and management but are now being expanded to other job categories.

• Allow people to try different jobs. Job testing is only one of the variables that needs to be considered when placing a person in a new position. Individual interest, the desire to learn, and a track record of success are also strong indicators of a person's ability to make a significant career change. We need to encourage people to try new jobs where they have no previous experience.

Miriam successfully moved from her position as manager of human resources training to manager of distribution for light and controls. For the first nine months, she inundated herself in the technology of lighting and controls. After an intense learning curve on technical issues, she set up an entirely new distribution system. Miriam was successful because she possessed excellent strategic thinking and communications skills and was able to learn technical aspects of the job. Initially, she experienced resistance from seasoned managers because she did not have twenty years of experience. But they began to support her when the distribution system she developed resulted in financial dividends to the company.

Too often we won't allow people to stretch this far from what they have done in the past.

Encouraging Individuals to Use Their Best Talents

Individuals need to accept the ultimate responsibility for placing themselves in jobs where they can contribute their best. Managers must help employees do this (as well as doing it themselves). There are three basic phases of change we go through in the process of developing our best talents:

1. Recognize the winds of change.
2. Find our joy.
3. Step into the unknown.

Phase One: Recognizing the Winds of Change

I believe in the statement "Do what you love and the money will follow." The problem is that what we we love changes over time. A job may fit us like a glove for years, and then suddenly it's not right anymore. It is uncomfortable and annoying when this happens because it is much easier to imagine staying where we are than facing the prospect of change.

Our emotions and experiences tell us when there is a change in the wind. Boredom, frequent illness, shortened temper, lack of energy, repeated failure, and even grief are signs that we need to make a change. When these signs occur, there are new interests that are trying to get our attention. If we listen to our feelings, internal nudging, and emerging interests, they will lead us to new possibilities and work situations that are more right for us.

I remember when I lost my desire to work. Over a period of six months, my interest in work completely left me. I drove to my office in tears because I didn't want to go there. I couldn't believe I didn't want to work anymore. I didn't want to facilitate a group, listen to skeptical employees, or help management plan a change process. I thought to myself, "What's the point? Nothing is going to change. I am wasting their time and mine." I lost hope that anything in the corporate world would ever change. This is a hard place for a change consultant to be. This was my work and I did not believe in it anymore. Work had lost its meaning.

During this time, a fellow consultant, Barbara Shipka, said to me, "Faith, you must engage with your work at a deeper level." At the time, I didn't have a clue what she meant. It took several months before her statement took on real meaning. Gradually, I began to see that my new work was to face the resistance I saw, to talk and write about it, and to help people address barriers to change in themselves. The process of finding a deeper purpose was full of waiting, anxiety, financial stress, self-doubt, disinterest in work, extreme highs and lows, and anything but comfort. The changes taking place inside of me were overwhelming and disconcerting. But I simply could not go forward without addressing my concerns.

Phase Two: Finding Our Joy

Work is meant to be an expression of who we are and what we have to contribute to the world. Too many of us work out of obligation, fear, and need. Few of us know how to work out of desire, love, and the sheer joy of using our talents. The closer we come to using our abilities, the closer we get to finding joy.

We need to offer what is our joy to give. When someone is wondering, "What do I want to be when I grow up?" my friend Jill Konrath asks the person this question: "What would you do for free?" In other words, what would you do even if no one pays you to do it?

Jill knows what she does for free. She is a natural sales coach. No matter where she goes or whom she is with, Jill is always coaching others on how to sell. She does it innately. As a sales professional, she began informally coaching her peers long before she was a sales manager. This is her gift to give. Yet it took her many years to recognize that this talent was what she should offer to her clients. Coaching was so easy for Jill that she considered it a sideline.

Our natural talents are sometimes difficult for us to see. They are an innate part of who we are and we make use of them with little effort. We don't see them as powerful gifts. Friends can see our talents better than we can. To define what we love to do, it is useful to ask friends and coworkers these two questions:

1. What am I really good at doing?
2. What do I do easily and often better than anyone else?

Clarity is important. When I am unclear about my work direction or purpose, I can call hundreds of clients and nothing comes of it. Yet when I know what I have to offer, clients seem to come out of nowhere. As we define our evolving interests and shape them into a job, we frequently discover that our new work magically combines many of the skills, interests, and connections we have developed over the years. The new work asks us to bring more of who we are to the table.

Janice is a dietitian who took time off to raise two young children. When she decides to return to work, she applies for jobs in the area of nutrition. After twenty interviews, she receives no offers. She decides to make a course correction. Janice asks herself, "What do I love to do? What is important to me? What am I really good at? What are my priorities?" She realizes she wants to work independently rather than as an employee. She wants to work as a consultant to organizations that need to come into compliance with state regulations. Janice decides to call herself a nutrition firefighter. Within two weeks of changing directions and moving closer to and clarifying her true interests and priorities, she has more work than she can handle. Earlier disappointments have helped Janice to discover, "Not this way—that way!"

Phase Three: Stepping Into the Unknown

There is no way to move into a new job or work situation without loosening our grip on what we currently have. Making the change requires that we let go of what makes us feel secure.

Sometimes when we have outgrown a job, it is mysteriously taken from us. When a job or position no longer fits us, it doesn't work for the organization either. We are laid off, the company goes out of business, or it sells the division we are working for. We wanted to change jobs, yet with white knuckles we held on to what we knew. The layoff is almost a relief. Now we have to step out. We have no choice.

Whether we are laid off or choose to leave, stepping into the unknown of a job search is rarely smooth or easy. There is a period of uncertainty, searching, evaluating, data gathering, and incubation before a decision or change is actually made. Sometimes, the first decision turns out to be wrong and we must regroup and begin again.

Making a change involves dealing with uncertainty. Halfway to our goal is the most dangerous point. We haven't reached our goal but we can't go back. This is a difficult spot and fortunately we don't have to stay there very long. Pretty soon, the light at the end of the tunnel emerges: The phone rings, an appointment gets scheduled, a new option emerges, and we are on our way to where we want to go. Answers come as we open up to questions, consider possible changes, and take actions to move forward. Our feelings assist us if we use them to turn our attention toward what excites us and brings us joy and renewed energy.

Engaging in a career change or reshaping our contribution at work is a courageous act. More of us are making these changes, and they are happening with increasing frequency. We need to talk openly about the process and how we are doing. The changes are not easy to make, and it is too lonely to do it alone. Hopefully, we will see the wisdom of supporting each other as we stretch, reach, and strive to become more of who we are and find new ways to contribute to our organizations.

ACTION EXERCISES

Exercise 1: Making Career Changes

The purpose of this exercise is to help you make a job or role change by learning from earlier experiences. This exercise is interesting to share with other people.

1. Recognize the need for change. Review changes you made in the past and describe how you knew it was time for a change.

   - Your internal feelings
   - The external events

2. How do you go about seeking a change?

   - Let it come to me
   - Poke around
   - Made a decision and move on it
   - Combination of the above

3. How did it feel to step into the unknown?

   - Initially
   - Midstream
   - When you landed in the new place

4. List what you learned from your experience that will help you now.

Exercise 2: Finding Your Joy

The purpose of this exercise is to help you identify what you love to do.

1. Ask yourself these questions:

   - What would you do for free?
   - Where do you donate your time?
   - What activities do you most enjoy doing?

2. Ask coworkers:

    • What do I do better than anyone you know?
    • What am I really good at doing?

    Make a list of these responses.

3. What jobs use these skills? Talk to others to find out.

Exercise 3: Supporting Career Development

The purpose of this exercise is to define ways organizations can support career and job change so that job requirements are aligned with individual and organizational needs. Answer the following questions:

1. How can we make it safe for individuals to discuss employment interests and concerns?
2. How can we support each other in finding positions that reflect our talents, interests, and priorities?
3. How can managers conduct layoffs without negatively affecting employee morale and motivation?
4. What activities can we initiate to assist individuals with career development? List specific ideas that you want to implement.

9

Gaining Commitment to Change

If we have never been there before, how do we know it's there?

—Maureen McGovern (at age 6),
daughter of Phil and Stephanie McGovern

Once upon a time, AT&T was the "only game in town." Customers and even employees remember the following as AT&T's attitude: "This is what we offer—take it or leave it. We make the rules. We are doing you a favor to provide this service."

Then deregulation occurred and a virtual revolution took place inside AT&T. Entitlement attitudes were gradually replaced with customer service attitudes; restrictive policies changed to respond to customer needs; bureaucratic structures were replaced with smaller, flexible work units; prices became negotiable and competitive; and marketing strategies became innovative. The need to survive dismantled sacred assumptions about what was possible. The customer now calls the shots.

To survive, organizations are implementing significant changes. Like AT&T, we are all challenged, not simply to develop new products and services, but to change our beliefs and behaviors as well. Customer demands for higher quality, lower cost, and improved service are changing the way we act and think.

Our business future depends on our ability to implement change.

- A government agency seeks to move away from enforcement into advising constituency.
- A medical company attempts to shrink time-to-market for new product introductions.
- An insurance company makes an acquisition to expand capabilities.
- A utility works to build community relations to ward off competitors.
- A mainframe computer business begins to sell integrated solutions.

Why Is Change So Difficult?

Over the past three decades, organizations have implemented a rash of programs to achieve the results they want. In the 1970s, the popular programs were participative management, culture change, and quality circles. In the 1980s, these initiatives were replaced with total quality management, empowerment, and process improvement. In the 1990s, the priorities are customer satisfaction, continuous improvement, reengineering, and team structures.

Employees react to new programs with skepticism. One manager tersely referred to his company's new quality initiative as the "program de jour." He says, "Our president recently talked to someone on an airplane and 'total quality' is now the new catchphrase." Employees affected by new initiatives say, "I really don't know *why* we are doing this. What are we really trying to accomplish? How does this effort fit with what we are already doing?" Underneath a thin veneer of compliance and involvement, skepticism and doubt run rampant.

A Poor Track Record

Our reputation for sustained commitment is not great. Many programs are abandoned or silently declared unsuccessful. Brilliant strategies never get off the ground. Empowerment efforts have their day in the sun and then disappear from existence.

- An electronics company forms customer-focused teams—only to watch them disintegrate as team recommendations conflict with current business practices.
- A communications company trains leaders to manage in innovative ways—then watches as implementation falters and profits decline.
- A new computer system is installed to revolutionize the business—and then is declared a failure when employees resist the technology and fail to implement procedures.

Words of commitment from management belie the reality of what takes place as efforts stumble and fade. We are like promiscuous lovers who run from one romance to the next, enchanted at first, then gradually disillusioned. Instead of looking at ourselves to find the source of the problem, we search for a new love that will work.

The Implementation Gap

Good ideas, whether generated at the top or initiated from the bottom, are difficult to implement. Despite our best efforts, new programs and strategies do not filter down or permeate the organization. Instead, we experience an implementation gap. If you are involved in a major change, check the following symptoms to assess whether this gap is occurring:

- Symptoms at the executive level

  _____ Do not walk the talk
  _____ Do not implement change as a team
  _____ Fail to communicate why the change is needed

- Symptoms at the middle management level

  _____ Lack enthusiasm for the change
  _____ Feel stretched beyond the limits of their capacity
  _____ Suffer bottleneck communication

- Symptoms at the employee level

  _____ Are in the dark about what is happening.
  _____ Feel skeptical and mistrustful.
  _____ Feel unheard, unappreciated, and underutilized.

The most insidious symptom is that no one believes a significant change is going to happen. The most common reason managers find themselves in this unproductive situation is that the grass roots of the organization are not sufficiently involved or empowered.

Closing the Gap and Succeeding at Change

Too often we declare the new program a failure *when it is we who have failed*. The following actions can be taken to close implementation gaps and ensure successful change:

- Keep going.
- Expand outdated assumptions.
- Learn from mistakes.
- Declare projects "dead."
- Be willing to say no.
- Integrate change with business as usual.
- Address personal concerns.

Let's examine each action.

Keeping Going

We need to keep going when we encounter problems. At the beginning of a new project, anything is possible: We make speeches, invest in consultants, engage in training, install systems, and have high hopes for what our investments will bring us. It's a time of optimism, new possibilities, learning, and anticipation that our problems will finally be fixed. Although stressful and anxious about the new endeavor, we are also full of hope.

Then the training sessions end, the new system is installed, the acquisition is made—and the reality of what we have done begins to take hold. The optimism we experienced begins to fade as difficult issues and challenges emerge. The system that was supposed to solve all our problems has major design flaws, the equipment we purchased to improve our production requires costly adjustments in personnel and schedules, and we discover unanticipated glitches in the acquisition. Real implementation has begun, and our bright hopes have turned into harsh demands for significant change. There is less hope and less support, and we must deal with difficult issues to make our investments pay off.

- A state agency gathers customer data and discovers that to respond to customer feedback, it must either drop or change half its programs.
- A medical company invests significant money in R&D for a new product. However, to launch the product, managers must give up 30 percent of their budget for the next year.
- An executive team reorganizes the business. However, the members realize that in order for the new structure to be effective, they need to address the trust issues among them.

This is when we balk because the changes now affect us personally! Moving forward can require us to give up power and control, adjust to a new way of doing something, let employees go and reduce budgets, alter the services we offer, address turf issues, spend money, move people to jobs that match their skills, and give up long-held beliefs. We need to keep going to achieve the results we want.

Expanding Outdated Assumptions

We must learn to expand our assumptions rather than give up on a project that is failing. At the beginning of a new project, we frequently underestimate what it will take to achieve the results we want.

A marketing department designs an innovative new product but the sales force can't sell it because the product is seen as a dud. In reality, the product might be just right for the company, but marketing has underestimated the amount of support, coaching, and training needed by the sales force to be successful. In another example, individuals in a high-tech company are trained to lead employee teams. They are expected to do their regular jobs as well as facilitate teams. But few of the facilitators have adequate time to work with the teams, and team efforts fail. Rather than declare the initiative a failure, management selects three individuals and gives them full-time responsibility for team facilitation.

Our early notions of what will work are not always right. We don't know what is needed until we get into the project. When problems emerge, we often need to expand our thinking rather than abandon the project.

Learning From Mistakes

We need to learn from mistakes instead of avoiding failure of any kind. When I confront my eight-year-old son about a problem, he says, "Let's not talk about it, Mom." This is what we do as adults: not talk about it. Mistakes are not good for our reputations or upward mobility. We believe people who make mistakes are sidelined, placed in staff jobs, and not taken seriously. We are lightning-quick at placing the blame rather than understanding what created the problem. But to avoid costly problems, we need to learn from our mistakes.

A high-tech company purchases a production facility so it does not have to outsource for parts. However, company managers do not have the background necessary to run the new venture. Very quickly, the acquisition starts to bleed profits away from the larger corporation. Finally after three years of heavy investment and many headaches, management decides the facility does not fit the core business and sells it. Later, this management team does a courageous thing. In a facilitated working session, the members review the situation and learn from the mistakes they made. Specifically, they discuss:

- The events that took place
- Key decisions that were made
- The rationale behind the decisions
- Personal needs and agendas involved

They identify key learnings, discuss problems and mistakes, and openly talk about actions to take in the future.

Declaring Projects "Dead"

A banking organization decides to train employees to work on teams. Numerous teams are formed, and work projects begin in earnest. Managers have secret doubts about whether the teams are moving fast enough, but they do not address their concerns openly. Privately, they resent the time employees are spending away from their departments. Gradually, fewer members come to the meetings, and without much being said, the team effort dies.

Some projects need to be dropped. However, it is the *way* we drop them that causes the problem. We pretend the project never happened. Instead, we need to address the issues, make go or no-go decisions, and communicate why the project is ending. Specifically, we need to:

- Announce the end of projects.
- Tell people why.
- Discuss what we learned.
- State what we will do differently in the future.

To address the teaming issues effectively in the banking organization, the managers would have expressed their concern about lack of progress, made a decision to disband or revitalize the teams, and actively communicated team status to employees and team members.

Being Willing to Say No

In organizational life, we learn quickly that it is more acceptable to say yes than it is to say no. Saying yes makes us a member of the team and shows that we are committed and willing to do whatever it takes to succeed. In contrast, saying no can brand us as uncooperative, unsupportive, uncommitted, and a naysayer. At the highest levels, the tendency to say yes to everything is one of the greatest contributors to implementation failures.

If we try to be all things to all people, we will have only marginal success. As a staff person in a public service organization complains:

> We say yes to everyone. We don't know what our priorities are. We are afraid to say no. The result is that we don't do anything well. Our reputation as an agency is on the line. Two major projects are not doing well because no one has the time for them. We come across as chaotic and unorganized.

To achieve focus, even good ideas must be turned down. We must dare to establish priorities and say no to projects that do not fit with our direction. We need to acknowledge and reinforce people for saying no. Statements we can use are:

> "That's a great idea, but right now these are our priorities."
> "We set limits on our services in order to do a few things well."
> "I'm glad you turned down that request because we need to focus on our priorities."

Integrating Change With Business as Usual

Success with implementation requires that we integrate new initiatives into the mainstream way of doing business. Too often we separate new initiatives from business as usual, teams are expected to perform without input from managers, employees are empowered and told to make decisions without necessary training and support, and change leaders are appointed but given inadequate support from management.

In a banking organization, the president appoints Clara as the director of quality. Clara participates in management meetings and gives monthly reports on progress under way. Training and recognition programs blossom under her leadership. However, managers do not integrate quality into daily activities or discussions. After two years, few tangible quality results are evident. The management team realizes that they have abdicated their responsibility for quality.

Putting inexperienced people in charge of new initiatives is like giving a baby a steak to eat. I often find women, minorities, and high-potential employees assigned to these risky jobs. It's a chance to prove themselves and, despite adverse circumstances, many of them do very well. But the downside is that the experienced leaders of the organization are not as involved as they need to be in the change.

Much good assessment and development work can be accomplished by lower-level teams, but their work can never replace the mainstreaming, legitimizing, and role modeling that needs to happen at the top. The leadership team must be willing to work directly on the changes they espouse. Specifically, leaders need to:

- Review progress on new initiatives at regular staff meetings.
- Assign an executive sponsor to support implementers.
- Communicate progress on initiatives to the rest of the organization.
- Take personal action that demonstrates visible commitment to the change.

Addressing Personal Concerns

Regardless of how positive a change might be, there are personal feelings and concerns. We worry about how the change will affect us. We sometimes ignore these feelings because they get in the way of moving ahead, but we need to allow our fears to surface and be addressed. The following list of concerns is adapted from material developed by change consultants Linda Ackerman Anderson and Dean Anderson.* Check the fears and concerns about work changes that you experience:

_____ Concerns about job and responsibilities

- Whom will I be reporting to?
- Will my work change?
- Is my job safe?

*Linda Ackerman Anderson and Dean Anderson, *Managing Change* (Durango, Colo.: Being First, 1990).

_____   Concerns showing resistance to change

- I don't like what's happening.
- I don't think this makes any sense at all.

_____   Concerns about winning or losing power

- Will I be a winner or a loser?

_____   Concerns about being out of control

- I want to have a say in what happens.

_____   Concerns about work load

- How can I do it all?
- How am I going to get my regular work done and this too?

_____   Concerns about competence and ability to implement

- I don't know if I can do this.
- I don't want to look like a fool.

_____   Concerns about safety and risk

- Do they really mean it?
- Is it safe to trust that this is going to happen?

We need to make it safe for individuals to express these concerns. If not, these concerns can sabotage what we are trying to accomplish. In meetings where new directions are being discussed, the leader can say, "Let's talk about the concerns and feelings that you have. How can we address them?" Once the concerns are expressed, they need to be accepted and responded to as honestly as possible. The following are guidelines for managers to follow when addressing employee concerns about change:

- Allow employees to have concerns without feeling that you have to fix the issues they bring up. You can't always.
- Be as honest as possible when you respond to employee

concerns. You may need to say, "There may be layoffs as a result of this change" or "I don't know the answer yet."

- Reassure employees that you will keep them up-to-date on the changes under way. Then do so.
- Welcome questions, suggestions, and input about the change.
- Engage employees in developing solutions to the issues that arise.

A Personal Commitment to Change

To implement change, we must move away from what we currently have toward what we want. This is not easy. We see what needs to be done, but somehow making the change isn't that simple. We take one step forward and three steps backward and wonder, "*Why* is change so difficult? Why is there so much resistance?"

Change is difficult because *all change is personal change*, requiring us to act and think differently. A large part of us may want to change but another part sabotages the change. Personal change is difficult because before we can move toward what we want, we must first journey through the self. No significant change can occur without honestly addressing the personal needs, beliefs, and feelings that keep us where we are.

Change requires internal alignment with the goals that we want to reach. Recognizing, accepting, and aligning our emotional needs and underlying beliefs with what we really want is the key to success. The more we recognize and acknowledge our current needs, beliefs, and feelings and make choices that are consistent with the desired results, the quicker change occurs. But if we deny, pretend, or ignore our true feelings, change will take longer.

There are three steps involved in aligning feelings with the changes that you want to make:

1. Journey to the self
2. Acceptance of needs and feelings
3. Change in attitudes and behaviors

Let's look at these steps in action.

Frank is the manager of the central processing unit in a large insurance company. His division is losing money because customer service is poor, competition is heating up, and expense is an issue. No one knows how to solve the problem.

Frank decides to pick up the gauntlet to fix the problem himself. He describes his decision to take action: "I took on the project as a personal mission. No one on the management team wanted to look at the situation—it was like rubbing their faces in cow piles to get them to talk about the issue." When Frank is asked why there was so much resistance to looking at the problem, he responds, "It was their cows that made the mess."

Frank empowers employees to find a solution to the problem after teaching them to make decisions by collecting facts, not opinions. Employees determine that the problem can be solved by centralizing the processing function. They recommend an aggressive plan to restructure the organization within fourteen months. Their recommendations are approved by upper management, and implementation begins in earnest. At this point, resistance to change starts to happen.

Department managers outside the division undercut Frank's employees by referencing policies and questioning their decisions. Frank finds himself at war with his peers and constantly defending the actions of his staff. He describes his personal style during this period as "combative, defensive, controlling, and highly protective" of his people. After nine months of struggling with managers who fight him every step of the way, Frank hits the wall. He asks himself, "Why am I doing this?" He is completely burned out.

Frank takes a step back and assesses his own feelings, needs, and beliefs about the situation. He is tired of fighting everyone, tired of doing it alone, and tired of defending his staff. He feels completely out of balance and depleted in his personal and work life.

At this point, Frank applies the three steps in his personal situation.

Journey to the Self

Our journey into new territory frequently includes hitting the wall. This is good because it forces us to examine ourselves.

As Frank reflects on his situation, he identifies the following:

1. My beliefs are:

   - I have the right answers.
   - I don't trust the other managers.
   - I have to fight this battle alone.
   - I must protect my staff.

2. My behaviors are:

   - I don't listen to the opinion of my peers.
   - I am defensive about what I am trying to do.
   - I have not involved other managers in the process.

3. My needs are:

   - I want my staff to be supported by other managers.
   - I want my staff to succeed with their mission.
   - I want to be supported by other managers.

Acceptance of Needs and Feelings

In our journey inward, it is important to *accept what we find*. Sometimes we discover resentments over past hurts that need to be addressed, anger at perceived inequity, and a yearning for support that is missing. We also find beliefs that are outdated, such as "I must do it alone" or "Others are not trustworthy." We need to accept how we feel before we can hope to change it. Once there is acceptance, we can choose which attitudes to keep and which to change.

Frank accepts that he does not listen to his peers or accept their views. His attitudes and behaviors have been control-oriented rather than participative. Frank starts to view his defensiveness as the loss of an opportunity to learn from other people.

Change in Attitudes and Behaviors

Frank begins to listen to what his peers have to say and implement some of their ideas. When the opportunity arises, he shares his opinions with them, but he does not push his ideas down anyone's throat. He starts to recognize what he can control and what he can only influence.

Frank's change in attitudes and behaviors begin to pay off. He has more energy at work. He stops seeing other managers as the enemy. And over time, he discovers that the other managers have many good ideas he was not considering. Tensions ease. His life comes into balance, and his employees are able to successfully implement the restructuring.

Summary

Real change happens when the part of us that wants to try, believe, and take a chance is bigger than the part of us that wants to resist, fight, sabotage, or pretend to be on board. We achieve commitment to change by learning to accept the needs, feelings, and beliefs that we encounter on the journey toward our goals. As we acknowledge the feelings of ourselves and others, we may elect to move ahead, stop, or go a different way. But whatever choice we make, we will not be pretending. Our actions will be authentic and we will move toward what we desire and believe in deeply.

ACTION EXERCISES

Exercise 1: Troubleshooting When Change Is Failing

The purpose of this exercise is to identify areas you might need to address if change is failing. Ask yourself and others the following questions about your project:

1. Is the change effort perceived as a priority?
2. Is there inadequate support for the change?
3. Do people know why the change is being implemented?
4. Do people outside the project know what is happening?
5. Are we seeking input from those who must adopt the change?
6. Are we helping people address their personal concerns about the change?
7. Has interest in the effort waned?
8. Is management involved and visibly committed?

Exercise 2: Dealing With Change

The purpose of this exercise is to help you align your internal needs with the external changes you want to make. Answer the following questions when you experience either internal or external resistance to a change:

1. Journey to the self

   - What do I like about the situation?
   - What do I dislike about the situation?
   - What concerns do I have?
   - What fears do I have?

2. Acceptance of needs and feelings

   - What feelings do I have about the situation?
   - What beliefs do I have about the situation?
   - What needs do I want to be addressed?
   - What behaviors do I wish were different?

3. Change in attitudes and behaviors
   - What outcomes do I want?
   - What actions can I take?
   - What attitudes can I change?

10

Revitalizing the Manager's Role

If you do what you've always done, you will get what you've always got.

—Ann Kaiser Stearns, *Coming Back*

Today, the role of the manager is changing as the business environment undergoes constant turmoil. Employees express frustration as they wait for managers to decide which strategy to pursue. Managers are frustrated as the directions they pursue look good one day and bad the next. Our ability to set a course and make clear, definitive decisions has diminished as we wade into complicated, interwoven problems.

Hiring outside experts to solve our business problems is proving to be less effective than it once was. Few experts can grasp the nuances of a corporate culture and make appropriate recommendations without enormous input from the people inside the organization. And just as cancer or heart disease cannot be cured by a single vaccine, so do business problems require multiple and integrated solutions. Answers can no longer come from one person, one company, or one government agency. We must find the solutions to complex problems by relying on each other's understanding and wisdom. The interdependence we now have on each other is significantly changing the manager's role.

Five New Roles for Managers

1. *The role of the manager is to coordinate the decision-making process.* Decision-making processes have become lengthy, convoluted, and time-consuming. Often, no one person has the authority to make a decision. Concurrent engineering, quality improvement, and just-in-time initiatives require people to be involved up front in decisions and throughout the process. The manager's role is to ensure timely input into decisions. This makes the manager's job much more complicated. Tidy, clean, insulated departments are exploding into full-blown community forums where everyone can voice his or her opinion about what the function should or shouldn't be doing. This highly interactive process is exciting and useful but not always comfortable for the manager who is used to having ultimate control over a department and decisions.

2. *The role of the manager is to build support for initiatives that last beyond his or her tenure.* In the past, one manager's pet project was often replaced when a new manager arrived. Although dismantling of programs still happens, it is too costly a proposition. Programs must outlast leaders. Managers realize the importance of implementing changes that last beyond their tenure. This means people must believe in the strategy or project rather than do it to please a specific boss.

3. *The role of the manager is to persuade and motivate rather than control and inspect.* Whether the reason is social or psychological, it is increasingly obvious that mandates don't work. For example, legislative decisions that impact education are highly dependent upon commitment from the schools themselves to be effective. There will never be enough money to ensure enforcement and compliance. In business, the manager's role is to gain buy-in and commitment for policies from individuals and groups that he or she doesn't control.

4. *The role of the manager is to build effective alliances and partnerships.* Groups of people who never imagined themselves in the same room together are now meeting to carve out solutions. Unions are working with management to save jobs, special interest groups are collaborating to secure funding, agencies are consolidating to save money, and competitors are cooperating to serve the

customer. Managers are charged with the task of ensuring the effectiveness of these partnerships and alliances.

5. *The role of the manager is to create high performing teams committed to a common goal.* Today, the manager is coordinating the work of specialists who report to other managers. The manager's team may be composed of individuals who have a history of competing with one another, come from diverse disciplines, have opposing views, and question the value of working together. This management responsibility is very different from leading a group of like-minded individuals who report solely to one person.

These trends are reshaping the role of the manager from:

Managing a function	to	Overseeing processes
Supervising work	to	Coordinating resources
Being the expert	to	Consulting with experts
Making decisions	to	Facilitating agreement
Enforcing regulations	to	Securing commitment
Giving the answers	to	Asking the questions

In short, the new role of the manager is to link, integrate, access, coordinate, and synthesize information from specialized areas in order to solve problems and respond to opportunities.

Implications for Managers

New attitudes, skills, and behaviors are required for the manager to step into this new role. The manager must be a master at dealing with people, understanding interpersonal dynamics and needs, gaining commitment, ensuring participation, leading groups, facilitating discussions, and resolving differences of opinion. To move into this role, the manager must frequently let go of the following outdated beliefs and attitudes.

"I must know everything." A manager becomes very nervous when his boss calls and asks for the details of a report. He frets,

"When my boss calls about a project, he expects me to have the answer immediately. I better know or be able to find out within the hour. But it's virtually impossible to let people make their own decisions and still know everything that's going on." Expecting managers to know all the details keeps us focused on a level of detail that is not beneficial to the organization.

"It's not my problem." The manager must assume responsibility for problems outside his or her span of control. Zed, a new products manager, takes credit when sales volume is up, but he also needs to feel equally responsible when the customer service department is swamped with complaints about the product. We must now take ownership of the whole, not just our part.

"I want immediate results." The issues we face will not be solved overnight. Lasting solutions can require months to implement. Too quickly, we become impatient with the laborious work of teams and involvement processes. The desire for immediate results affects the way we spend our time. We are attracted to fire fighting and operational issues because we can see tangible results. But we must loosen our grip on quick fixes or we will still be handling today's problems tomorrow.

The following are six skills and behaviors that are required in the new management role:

1. Balancing being gone from with being in the office.
2. Motivating people who don't report to us.
3. Creating a climate where it's safe to tell the truth.
4. Addressing emotional concerns.
5. Communicating early and often.
6. Leading highly productive meetings.

Balancing Being Gone From With Being in the Office

There are two extreme management behaviors that need to be brought into balance. One extreme is the manager who is always gone from the office, out discovering new ideas and making contacts—but is never in the office long enough to integrate these ideas into the way business is conducted. The opposite extreme is the manager who is always in the office, closing out new ideas and specializing in knowing everything that is going on.

We must strike a balance in our contact with the outside world. I have a friend who cleans his own house even though he has enough money to hire a housekeeper. He is a very busy person, so I asked him why he does it. He replied, "Cleaning my house is how I know what's going on. If I don't clean it, I completely lose touch with what needs to be fixed and how things are working." This is similar to the approach we need to have toward management responsibilities: gone enough to gather new ideas, meet people, and make important connections, but also there enough to know what is going on and see what needs to be done.

In our absence, we must give employees strong values and information that enable them to make the right choices whether we are there or not.

Motivating People Who Don't Report to Us

To gain commitment to change, the manager must communicate to employees, customers, and stakeholders in ways that are compelling and believable. The manager must know how to sell solutions, handle resistance, communicate in nonthreatening ways, and gain buy-in from diverse groups. The manager must also be able to form bonds among individuals who come from different backgrounds and technical specialties.

Creating a Climate Where It Is Safe to Tell the Truth

The manager needs to assume responsibility for making it safe for people to tell the truth. The truth for one person is different from the truth for another. Multiple points of view need to be encouraged and respected. To accomplish this, the manager can:

- Ask individuals for their ideas and suggestions.
- Probe when people hint that there is a problem.
- Let employees know their views are heard and appreciated.
- Listen to feedback even when it is poorly communicated.
- Conduct listening sessions to gather information.

- Lead skip-level meetings where both managers and employees learn information and ask questions.
- Challenge those who always agree to disagree!

Addressing Emotional Concerns

Change is volatile. People react to it with anger, mistrust, tears, and repressed emotions. The manager needs to be able to walk into a room of angry employees, listen to their points of view, acknowledge their feelings, and genuinely respond to their concerns—even when the answers are not what they want to hear. Tensions that are avoided do not go away! If a manager can facilitate these situations in a constructive way, the chances of success on a project are much higher.

Communicating Early and Often

When I was growing up, my mother always used to say, "No news is good news." Too many managers have this communication philosophy as well. The only time employees hear about a change from their manager is after the decision is made. What is "in the wind" is rarely discussed. The belief is: "We don't want to upset people or deal with unnecessary speculation." If employees were truly unaware of what was happening, this might be a possibility, but they are very aware.

Managers must learn to talk about difficult issues before they are decided and give employees time to discuss and understand the implications. This means no more one-way communication meetings. Involving employees in changes and decisions must be done early and often. Too much time and energy is squandered by employee guessing and speculation. If leaders tap this energy, they can use it to gain buy-in, solicit implementation ideas, and gain commitment to change early in the process.

Leading Highly Productive Meetings

Managers spend 90 percent of their time in meetings. Meetings are an organization's most precious use of time. Every person present represents time and money that needs to be honored by the way a meeting is run. But most managers dread meetings. Too much time is spent listening to the dominant person's point of view, discussing issues with no follow-through, talking about details that are unimportant, and reporting on projects with no meaningful discussion. Meetings can become highly ritualized events, designed to keep anything controversial from coming to the surface.

Meetings need to become places where the real issues are discussed, creative options are explored, agreements are reached, decisions are made, and actions are decided upon. Much help is available to improve meeting effectiveness. The following simple changes can bring immediate improvement.

- Set an agenda.
- Start the meeting on time.
- Allow time for discussion.
- Vary the format.
- Rotate the leadership.
- Record important decisions.

Meetings are used to achieve many different outcomes. Use the following checklist to clarify the outcomes you want to achieve in your meetings:

___ Solicit input and ideas about a problem.
___ Communicate information and ensure understanding.
___ Help the group or person reach a decision.
___ Explore new options and solutions.
___ Determine the best solution to a problem.
___ Gain commitment to act in new ways.
___ Encourage differences of opinions.
___ Resolve differences of opinions.
___ Reach consensus on a decision.
___ Learn new information.
___ Critique a proposal and give feedback.
___ Understand why something is not working.

Make sure individuals know the role you want them to play at different times in the meeting. Specify whether you want them to:

- Generate new ideas.
- Listen and understand.
- Make a decision.
- Critique and give feedback.

Another simple yet highly effective process that can be used to improve meeting and group effectiveness is a plus and minus chart. At the end of a meeting, group members write their responses to three questions on a flip chart:

1. In this meeting, I liked (+) the following (procedures, behaviors, attitudes, beliefs, achievements, etc.).
2. In this meeting, I disliked (—) the following (procedures, behaviors, attitudes, beliefs, etc.).
3. In our next meeting, we will make the following changes and take these actions.

Much help is available to improve meeting effectiveness. Managers can use video feedback, engage a process consultant, take time to self-critique, and even use computerized decision-making technology. We need to stop tolerating ineffective meetings, realize the opportunity present, and resist the norm that says, "We've always done it this way."

The Need for Facilitation Skills

To meet these challenges, the modern manager needs the skills of facilitation—people skills—as much as the shoemaker of old needed a hammer. It is virtually impossible to address opposing points of view, encourage differences of opinions, handle emotional reactions, create synergy among separate individuals, discuss issues that impact job security, build a team out of strangers, and gain commitment to decisions without facilitation skills. The ability to facilitate is a fundamental underpinning for modern management. But most managers are not trained in facilitation skills and find that using them feels strange and awkward at first.

The following are two different skill sets needed by the manager in his or her new role: skills for problem-solving issues and facilitation skills for dealing with people. Both are necessary.

Problem-Solving Skills

1. Understand the problem by asking:

   - What is the situation?
   - What are the issues?
   - What is the data?

2. Identify the vision and goals by asking:

   - What needs to be changed?
   - What are our goals?
   - What are measures of success?

3. Implement solutions by asking:

   - How do we implement?
   - Whom do we involve?

4. Continuously improve by asking:

   - Are we making progress?
   - What can we improve?

Facilitation Skills

1. Form the team by:

   - Communicating the need
   - Gaining commitment
   - Clarifying roles

2. Empower people by:

   - Ensuring participation
   - Creating a safe environment
   - Building trust

3. Resolve conflicts by:

  - Creating win-win solutions
  - Facilitating differences

4. Gain buy-in and commitment by:

  - Creating buy-in for change
  - Addressing resistance

Problem-solving skills need to work hand in hand with facilitation skills. Rarely are managers trained adequately in both sets of skills.

The following are indicators that problem-solving tools are necessary. Members of the group:

- Skip to solutions too quickly.
- Fail to challenge underlying assumptions.
- Settle for limited solutions.
- Focus on internal needs, not customer needs.
- Manage by opinions, not facts.
- Attempt to fix everything at once.

The following are indicators that facilitation skills are necessary. Members of the group:

- Feel negated and ignored.
- Function as individuals, not as a team.
- Are afraid to tackle the real issue.
- Blame others for problems.
- Don't trust each other.
- Can't resolve conflicts.

Use of problem-solving skills alone leads to sterile analysis and neglect of interpersonal issues that affect teamwork and trust, whereas use of facilitation skills alone produces a warm sense of bonding but fails to provide adequate analysis, understanding, and solution of the issues.

The Magnitude of the Change

We underestimate what is required to make even modest changes in our management style. Changing our expectations and assumptions about the manager's role is a revolution, not an evolution of what we do today. Old habits die hard and some of them are necessary. The manager is caught in the transition to a new management style.

The greatest amount of support for change in the manager's role is needed at the top. Changes in management style made at the executive level will permeate the organization, whereas changes in individual style tend to remain in isolated pockets. A fundamental truth in organizations is: *We tend to manage as we are managed.*

We can no longer expect managers to treat employees in ways that we ourselves are not treated. Nor can we expect managers to change simply because we are paid well. Money cannot replace the need for support. We do not outgrow our need for practice, encouragement, and support when making a significant change.

We would like to believe we are capable of swallowing this elephant in one bite, but this is not possible. We may want to go to one big event and have it change us forever, but overcoming decades of traditional management behaviors will take time. Behavior change requires bite-size bits of knowledge and skill practice over time to become a way of life. Anything less is simply motivational or awareness training and will fall away within weeks. Successful programs designed to help individuals achieve significant change—such as Weight Watchers, Alcoholics Anonymous, athletic training, language schools, and music lessons—require consistent practice, support, and application over an extended period of time. *There is no quick fix.*

A Worthy Investment

To move into new roles, managers need to engage in regular, ongoing doses of skills development and discussions about how management skills can be applied to daily work activity. Management teams need to become virtual support groups for transforming assumptions and behaviors—places where new skills are learned, information is shared, assumptions are challenged, concerns are expressed, and experiences are shared. Managers can benefit by learning from each other's successes and failures.

One hour a week or two hours every other week is a minimal investment to make to transform management skills. Commitment to a year of learning is a realistic expectation for change to occur. We readily make this type of commitment to the adoption of new software programs and production technology. Now it is time to make this commitment to our own development. Skilled managers who can provide leadership for the future are the most valuable asset we have.

ACTION EXERCISES

Exercise 1: Clarifying the Manager's Role

The purpose of this exercise is to identify changes in your role as a manager and reach agreement with others about the future direction of your role.

1. Mark your expectation of your role as a manager on the continuum below. [**0** = no expectation; **10** = great expectation]

   | Manage a function | to | Oversee processes |
   0_____**10**

   | Supervise work | to | Coordinate resources |
   0_____**10**

   | Be the expert | to | Consult with experts |
   0_____**10**

   | Make decisions | to | Facilitate agreement |
   0_____**10**

   | Enforce regulations | to | Secure commitment |
   0_____**10**

   | Give the answers | to | Ask the questions |
   0_____**10**

2. Ask your manager to mark your priorities on the same continuum.
3. Discuss differences in expectations and how your role is changing.
4. Agree on your current role and the direction of your role.
5. Discuss implications for training and skills development.

Exercise 2: Receiving Feedback on Management Style

The purpose of this exercise is to receive feedback on your management practices from employees and others. (Feel free to add items to the following list.)

1. Ask individuals at work to rate you on how well you:

   • Balance being gone from with being in the office

- Motivate people who don't report to you
- Create a climate where it's safe to tell the truth
- Address emotional concerns
- Communicate early and often
- Lead highly productive meetings

2. Identify changes you want to make based on this feedback.

Exercise 3: Practicing Facilitation Skills

The purpose of the exercise is to practice the use of facilitation skills to both understand an issue and decide on solutions.

1. To fully understand an issue, use the behaviors listed on the left. To reach agreement about solutions, use the behaviors listed on the right. Always summarize the discussion after you understand the issue and after you decide on solutions.

Understanding the Issue	Deciding on Solutions
I ask	I propose
I listen	I suggest
I discover	I inform
I assess	I specify
I understand	I conclude
I delve into	I agree

2. Notice and then comment on how it feels to fully understand the problem before talking about solutions.

Exercise 4: Applying Facilitation Skills

The purpose of this exercise is to apply facilitation skills to the solution of a problem. The following are a series of questions that managers can use to help a person or team discover the solution to an issue being addressed:

1. Understanding the situation

   - What is the situation?
   - What are the facts about the situation?
   - What are your opinions about the situation?
   - What are your feelings about the situation?

2. Identifying the problem

   - What problem exists?
   - What isn't working as well as it could?
   - What frustrations are you encountering?

3. Clarifying the implication

   - What are the consequences of this not working?
   - What could possibly happen if this continues?
   - What are the benefits of changing things?

4. Deciding on action needed

   - What changes are needed?
   - What specific changes do you want to make?

Index